Gospel of God's Grace and His Kingdom

Insights and Reflections

Eva Peck

© 2022 by Eva Peck
All rights reserved
Except for any fair dealing permitted under the Copyright Act, no part of this book may be reproduced by any means without prior permission of the author and publisher.

Cover graphic: PrimoCollection - DigiProductImages.com
Cover design: Eva Peck
Author photo: Alex Peck

Bible quotes, unless otherwise indicated, are taken from the *Holy Bible, New International Version*. Copyright © 1973, 1978, 1984 by International Bible Society. Used by permission of Zondervan Publishing House. All rights reserved.

ISBN: 978-0-9876279-3-3

A catalogue record for this book is available from the National Library of Australia

The book can be purchased online through
http://www.pathway-publishing.org.
Also available at Amazon, Ingram, and other outlets worldwide.

Dedicated to
our Loving Heavenly Father
— the God of Grace —
and all His children.

Other Books by the Author

Divine Reflections in Times and Seasons
Divine Reflections in Natural Phenomena
Divine Reflections in Living Things
Divine Insights from Human Life
Jesus' Gospel of God's Love
The Greatest Love
Salvation
Who and What Is God?
The Problem of Evil
Life after Death
Answers to Prayer
The Bible as a Guide to Life
Fulfillment of Old Testament Types
Nature of Soul and Spirit
Discerning Truth and Divine Guidance
Antidote to Fear and Anxiety – Fear of God
Abundant Living on Small Income

Co-author of:
Pathway to Life – Through the Holy Scriptures
Journey to the Divine Within – Through Silence, Stillness and Simplicity
Jesus Christ – A New Look at His Identity and Mission
Realities of Life – Reflections in Verse

For more information, see Pathway Publishing, www.pathway-publishing.org

For free downloads, go to
https://universal-spirituality.net/about/free-publications/

Acknowledgements

First, I would like to thank the Great God, our heavenly Father, as well as my spirit guides and teachers for enabling, inspiring, and blessing this book.

I wish to thank my dear husband Alex for his unfailing love and ever-present help and support behind the scenes.

In addition to the Bible and inspired information channelled by James Padgett, Daniel Samuels, as well as others, I also acknowledge drawing on the expertise of other experts on spiritual matters as needed -- see Specific References in the back of the book.

I am grateful to my friends who have been encouraging me in my gift of writing.

Without God's inspiration and the support and encouragement of the above-mentioned dear souls, this book would not have become what it is. So heartfelt thanks to all.

Contents

Preface v
PART I – WHAT IS GOD LIKE? 1
Nature of God 3
The God of Grace 8
Experience of Grace.. 12
PART II – GOSPEL OF GOD'S GRACE............................ 17
Gospel of God's Grace and His Kingdom 19
How Is the Gospel of Grace the Full Will of God 26
Paul's Experience of God's Saving Grace....................... 29
False and True Grace.. 38
Reflection on the Gospels.. 41
PART III – NEW BIRTH: ITS ASPECTS......................... 51
New Birth.. 53
God in Us and We in Him 56
Becoming At-One with Father 61
Christ in Us 64
The Counsellor / Spirit of Truth / Holy Spirit................. 67
PART IV – THE HOLY SPIRIT... 75

What Else Can We Learn About the Holy Spirit? 77

Holy Spirit and Divine Love 83

Relationship of God, Jesus, the Christ and Holy Spirit ... 89

PART V – ACCESSING GOD'S LAVISH GRACE 95

If You Understand the Gospel of Grace 97

Prayers for Divine Love 99

Epilogue 105

References 107

About the Author 110

About Pathway Publishing 112

Preface

This book was originally inspired by Paul's farewell address to the Ephesian elders on his way to Jerusalem (Acts 20:24-27).

Ac 20:24 However, I consider my life worth nothing to me, if only I may finish the race and complete the task the Lord Jesus has given me—the task of testifying to *the gospel of God's grace.*

Ac 20:25 "Now I know that none of you among whom I have gone about *preaching the kingdom* will ever see me again.

Ac 20:26 Therefore, I declare to you today that I am innocent of the blood of all men.

Ac 20:27 For I have not hesitated to *proclaim to you the whole will of God.*

Here Paul refers to the gospel he received from Jesus as the gospel of God's grace and "preaching the kingdom". He also equates these with "the whole will of God". How is the gospel of God's grace and of the Kingdom "the whole will of God"?

So the book addresses three questions:

1. What is God's grace?
2. How is grace connected to the kingdom?
3. How is the gospel of God's grace and of the Kingdom "the whole will of God"?

First, however, we briefly explore the nature of God – the God of grace – based on the Bible, other reading, and personal insights. Four volumes of mediated messages received about 100 years ago, now published under the title, *True Gospel Revealed Anew by Jesus*, that complement the Bible are drawn on in specific instances.

The danger of false or misunderstood grace is also looked at, as is Paul's dramatic awakening to grace.

Part Three deals with specific aspects of the gospel of grace. It examines in several chapters the new birth and what this process entails, how the Holy Spirit works in our lives, what is becoming our relationship with the Father, Jesus, the Christ, and the Spirit.

Part Four further expands on the nature and working of the Holy Spirit, the vital player in the transformation process which imparts Divine Love and substance to human souls.

The last part shows how each of us can avail ourselves of God's lavish offer of abundant grace that will place us on the path to salvation, being born again or from above, and achieving our destiny which is an incredible future in God's Celestial Kingdom for all eternity. Example prayers for God's Divine Love – the key element on the journey to salvation are included, both from the Bible and elsewhere.

The book is to some extent a collection of independent writings and reflections on the theme. Therefore each chapter can stand on its own and there may be some overlap and repetition. There is however, also flow and continuity.

Readers are encouraged to consider what is presented, some of which may be new to them, decide for themselves if it resonates and then act accordingly.

"To him who is able to do immeasurably more than all we ask or imagine, according to his power that is at work within us, to him be glory in the church and in Christ Jesus throughout all generations, for ever and ever! Amen." (Ephesians 3:20-21)

Eva Peck
December 2021

PART I – WHAT IS GOD LIKE?

Nature of God

This chapter draws on the Bible and another source of revelation that I have come to appreciate, *True Gospel Revealed Again by Jesus*, as far as exploring the nature of God.

God is Soul, composed of His greatest attribute, Divine Love, which is His very nature and essence, followed by mercy, goodness, power, omniscience, and will (1 John 4:8, 16[1]; Psalm 116:12; Deut. 4:31; Eph. 2:4-5[2]). The mind, so much worshipped by humankind, is only one aspect of His Being. God as Soul is far more than the sum of all His attributes.

God's attributes radiate from His great Soul and flood the universe. So, when people say they live and have their being in God (Acts 17:28), they are technically in error, but they do live and have their being in the divine attributes that emanate from God and that He has placed in their human soul. God has a place in the Celestial Heavens, but His attributes are everywhere and fill the whole universe, or multiple universes that scientists postulate might exist. The earth is a tiny portion of the entire universe. Even the "heaven" or spirit world where humans go when they die is a subset of the entirety of Creation (Psalm 47:8[3]; 53:2; 139:7-13[4])

Although God has no form or shape such as He gives to humans on incarnation, nor a spirit body such as that manifested by humans after their physical death, God does possess a Soul form. However, He cannot be seen with the physical or spiritual sight, but can only be perceived with the soul's eyes opened by the influence of the Divine Love. God's form, or its divine attributes, becomes more clearly perceptible to the human soul as it comes into a closer rapport with God. This happens as a result of its development and transformation through the Divine Love (Matt. 5:8; John 3:3; 1 John 3:1-2 [5]).

While God is Soul, alone and unique in its oneness, and while He has no material or spirit body, He has personality – divine personality manifesting His Love, kindness and solicitude for all His creatures. God is a God of Love, above all else. He is not a God of hatred, nor does He chastise His children in wrath or anger. His love is for all humanity, be they saints or sinners, and no one suffers punishment because the Father wants them to suffer. He is a God of mercy and forgiveness, and will forgive the sins of those who in sincerity ask Him (Isa. 55:7[6]).

God, then, is not a cold intellect, an abstract mind, or an indifferent and unfeeling force, but rather a personal, warm and loving Father / Mother, eager for the happiness of His children, regardless of their race, colour or creed. The real truth and understanding of God is beyond the comprehension of the finite mind, and can only be accepted as a realization of an existing truth by means of faith.

No one has ever seen God, for God cannot be seen as described in some of the Bible stories. God generally works through His angels (Heb. 1:14), rather than directly. So His angels and messengers were seen, spoke to the prophets, and represented themselves as angels of God. Jesus was God's chosen son to do the work of redeeming the earth from sin, and came as his Father's representative. He never was God, nor did he claim to be (Mark 10:17-18).

No man has heard the voice of God, for He has no voice. The "voice of God" that spoke to the disciples on the Mount of Transfiguration, and to John and those at Jesus' baptism, was actually the voice of one of God's highest angels. Other than communicating through angels or inspired writings, God works in a silent, mysterious way, through communication from His Soul to human souls.

Through His ministering angels, God seeks to turn His children to Him and have them keep in harmony with His laws in developing their natural love, or obtain at-onement with Him through the inflowing of His Divine Love into their souls in response to their earnest prayers. A person can become at-one with the Father to the extent that His Love abounds in their soul. This was what Jesus prayed for in one of his last prayers on earth (John 17:20-23).

Sample Bible passages in support of the presented concepts:

(1) 1 John 4:8, 16: Whoever does not love does not know God, because God is love. ... And so we know and rely on the love God has for us. God is love. Whoever lives in love lives in God, and God in him.

(2) Ephesians 2:4-5: But because of his great love for us, God, who is rich in mercy, made us alive with Christ even when we were dead in transgressions — it is by grace you have been saved.

(3) Psalm 47:8: God reigns over the nations; God is seated on his holy throne.

(4) Psalm 139:7-12: Where can I go from your Spirit? Where can I flee from your presence? If I go up to the heavens, you are there; if I make my bed in the depths, you are there. If I rise on the wings of the dawn, if I settle on the far side of the sea, even there your hand will guide me, your right hand will hold me fast. If I say, "Surely the darkness will hide me and the light become night around me," even the darkness will not be dark to you; the night will shine like the day, for darkness is as light to you. For you created my inmost being; you knit me together in my mother's womb.

(5) 1 John 3:1: How great is the love the Father has lavished on us, that we should be called children of

God! And that is what we are! The reason the world does not know us is that it did not know him. Dear friends, now we are children of God, and what we will be has not yet been made known. But we know that when he appears, we shall be like him, for we shall see him as he is.

(6) Isaiah 55:7: Let the wicked forsake his way and the evil man his thoughts. Let him turn to the LORD, and he will have mercy on him, and to our God, for he will freely pardon.

The God of Grace

In nearly fifty New Testament passages, God is associated with grace. This article explores why is God a God of grace.

God embodies and personifies love and grace. Even in the Old Testament, He is described as loving, forgiving, gracious, compassionate, merciful, as well as slow to anger and punishment (Neh. 9:17, 31; Ps 86:15; 103:8; 111:4; 116:5; 145:8; Isa 30:18; Joel 2:13; Jonah 4:2)

The God of grace makes His general grace universally available throughout the creation in the form of life sustenance, provision, renewal, and special blessings for all creatures and people of all nations (Neh. 9:6; Job 5:10; 24:5; 25:3; 36:31; 38:41; 65:9; Ps 147:9; Isa 55:10).

In addition to the above-mentioned general grace of God's provision and help (2 Cor 9:8; 12:9), the New Testament refers to a special grace brought by Jesus Christ (John 1:14-17) and offered to all who are receptive.

It appears from both experience and scripture that some people are more spiritually inclined than the majority. Perhaps those the Father has drawn or called to become Jesus' followers and disciples (John 6:44). This being "chosen" – or helped to choose God's way – occurs by grace, without any merit of the individual involved. It is a free and unearned gift (Rom 11:5-6) and involves an opportunity to embark on a way to salvation through transformation by divine love, imparted through the Holy Spirit, which is free for the asking (Rom. 5:5; Tit 3:4-7).

Of course, free will on the part of humans is involved at all times. Those who desire and accept these gifts of saving grace then need to cultivate soul growth and development in their lives, and follow the leading of the Holy Spirit which imparts God's Divine Love and nature. They need to "walk in the Spirit" and love God and others as Jesus loved — with the Divine Love that transcends the natural human love they are born with (John 13:34, 15:12, Rom. 5:5; Gal. 5:16, 25; Eph. 5:2, 8, 18; 2 Pet 1:4).

In the context of saving grace, the Bible shows that this grace includes:
The message of the gospel
God's intervention in the lives of those who are called to discipleship
Response to God's call
God's way of life
Means of justification, sanctification, salvation, and eternal life
The present redeemed state of believers
Personal spiritual gifts and responsibilities
(Acts 11:23; 13:43; 15:11; 18:27; 20:24, 32; Rom 3:24; 5:2, 21; Eph 1:7; 2:5-8; 3:2-8; 4:7; 2 Tim 1:9; 1 Pet 4:10; 5:10.)

According to *The New Dictionary of Catholic Spirituality*, in an article entitled "Grace" by Robert Haight (p. 452-464), grace is:

A gift of God
Forgiveness
Love and favor
God's initiative of salvation
God's merciful response to sin and death
God's personal self-communication to humans
God's indwelling – that is, a person's union with God
Fully gratuitous – free, unowed, unearned, and undeserved

The following passages show more specifically how saving grace is special, and occurs in addition to the general grace available to all humanity and in which, through the omnipresent Spirit of God, "we live and move and have our being" (Acts 17:26-28).

Those graced with the saving grace have the opportunity to be the first-fruits of salvation (Eph 1:3-14; Jas 1:18; Rev 14:4). They have been enlivened from being spiritually dead in sins and their eyes have been opened to God's special revelation (Eph 2:4-10; Mt 13:11-17; 16:16-17, 20; 1 Cor 1:21-24). They have been drawn by the Father, shown their sinful and alienated state, and called to repentance, reconciliation, and ultimately oneness with God through the Divine Love of the Father imparted by the Holy Spirit

(Jn 6:44, Acts 2:38-41; Rom 5:5, 8-11; 2 Cor 5:18-20; Eph 2:12-20; Col 1:19-22).

Through the Holy Spirit imparting God's Divine Love and nature into their souls, they have entered into the special grace and become God's true and redeemed children, born of the Spirit (Jn 1:9-13; 3:5-16; 1 Pet 1:1-5, 23). All this is entirely God's doing and grace – without any human merit except for faith and acceptance of the divine invitation (Rom 3:21-28; Eph 2:8-9; 2 Tim 1:8-10; Tit 3:5). The Holy Spirit is a guarantee of divine adoption or new birth as children of God and of future glory and immortality in God's Celestial Kingdom (Rom 8:9-17, 22-23; 1 Cor 15:50-57; Mt 24:30-31).

So, indeed, God can truly be seen as a God of grace. Firstly, grace given to all human and non-human creatures in providing them with life and sustenance. With Jesus' coming, humanity received the opportunity for a new and special grace first offered to and rejected by the first humans. This offer was to receive and be transformed by God's Divine Love and nature resulting in glory and immortality. God commissioned Jesus, the first human to embark on this new journey of grace. He and his followers were commissioned to preach the gospel of grace, which is also the gospel of the Kingdom of God and encompasses the whole will of God (Acts 20:24-27).

Experience of Grace

Truth about God is revealed to humans through personal experience, through the universe and nature, and through divine revelation that surpasses experience. Here are some examples of experiencing God in life.

Many faith traditions, including those outside of Christianity, have the concept of a higher Spirit power. Without this belief, life has no meaning and becomes purely a very temporary existence of ceaseless striving and purposeless suffering with an inevitable end in death. Humans feel by nature insecure, trying to justify and find meaning in their existence. The concept of death – being reminded that we don't have to be and will one day cease to be – fosters a continual fear which is a chronic pain. Life by itself is futile, no matter what we accomplish or accumulate.

Something in the human heart, soul and psyche is yearning for more than this. Human beings with their potential for fantastic creativity, ability to conceptualize amazing ideas and bring into existence incredible things, as well as being able to display great altruism and self-sacrifice can also experience a great restlessness and descend to tremendous depths of depravity. Why this paradox? And is there anything behind all this as well as behind special moments from beyond ourselves –

experiences of transcendence or what could be called "moments of grace"?

Most of us, if we stop and think, have experienced amazing synchronicities or coincidences as well as unexplainable favourable happenings that have become a special and undeserved gift -- a gift of grace. Sometimes we may only realize retrospectively that something extraordinary had occurred. These experiences can be both positive and negative -- experiences of limitation in which our world falls apart and, in our powerlessness, we become open to mystery and grace.

The *positive experiences of transcendence* and awareness that what is given cannot be attributed to ourselves include interpersonal love, childbirth, creativity, forgiveness, and the beauty of nature. They also include supernatural protection when disaster was certain, and special breakthroughs when things came together just at the right time without our effort.

For example, the love shared by a man and a woman in marriage, or even between friends, is something profound, undeserved, wonderful, and mysterious. Likewise, experiencing or witnessing the birth of one's own child often gives the parents an overwhelming sense of the mystery of life – sensing that they are co-creators of the new and unique human being with Something that is beyond them and that the child is a special gift given to them and in a way, not totally theirs.

In creative endevours of any kind, we often sense inspiration – being touched from within and sensing the mystery of our own being as well as something beyond us which accounts for what we have produced. Other moments of grace occur when the heart is supernaturally softened and we are enabled to let go of anger and bitterness and forgive the person who has grievously wronged us. Also, something marvelous and overpowering in nature gives us a sense of personal smallness and an awesome mystery beyond, which often elicits thanksgiving and praise.

Experiences of grace in limiting situations include disaster, death, failure, terminal illness, loneliness, and alienation. In these we hit our limits and finiteness, yet as it happens, we are taken beyond ourselves into the mystery of grace. In our darkest hours, we may, perhaps for the first time, cry out for help to a Higher Power – having exhausted all our options and hoping against hope that someone may hear and answer. And often, there is a sense of being helped, upheld, and supported. While difficult to deal with at the time, these experiences may ultimately become life-giving turning points.

If we become mindful and attuned to these moments of grace – even in small, ordinary things and events, we'll be amazed and indeed awed at their frequency. It is all a matter of awareness.

Another aspect of divine grace transcends the physical and mundane as our eyes become opened to realities beyond the here and now and beyond death. We become awakened to our spiritual state and start asking about the purpose of our lives and how to fulfill it both in this life and beyond. We realize our shortcomings and the need to rise above our human condition. And we may start seeking and be led to the way to "salvation" -- a spiritual life transformation in this life in order to ultimately fulfill our God-given purpose in the life beyond here. This is the greatest of all of God's gifts of grace and results in the God of grace transforming us by giving us of His substance and nature to become His true children and enjoy immortality in His Celestial Kingdom. This is God's salvation, all free for the asking, but requiring desire, commitment and conscious effort on our part.

(Some ideas were adapted from *Human Experience of God*, Denis Edwards.)

PART II – GOSPEL OF GOD'S GRACE

Gospel of God's Grace and His Kingdom

In a farewell address to the Ephesian elders on his way to Jerusalem, Paul refers to the gospel he received from Jesus as "the gospel of God's grace", "preaching the kingdom" and "proclaiming the whole will of God."

Ac 20:24 However, I consider my life worth nothing to me, if only I may finish the race and complete the task the Lord Jesus has given me—the task of testifying to *the gospel of God's grace.*

Ac 20:25 "Now I know that none of you among whom I have gone about *preaching the kingdom* will ever see me again.

Ac 20:26 Therefore, I declare to you today that I am innocent of the blood of all men.

Ac 20:27 For I have not hesitated to *proclaim to you the whole will of God.*

Let's look at each of these three aspects of the gospel and unwrap their rich meaning.

What Is Grace?

The word is used more than 100 times in the New Testament. Here are some things we can learn about grace:

Grace is something unearned or undeserved – a gift.

Eph 2:8-9 — For it is by grace you have been saved, through faith —and this not from yourselves, it is the gift of God—not by works, so that no one can boast.

2Ti 1:9 [God] has saved us and called us to a holy life—not because of anything we have done but because of his own purpose and grace.

Grace relates to God's love and mercy.

Eph 2:4-5 But because of his great love for us, God, who is *rich in mercy*, made us alive with Christ even when we were dead in transgressions—*it is by grace you have been saved.* ...

Eph 2:7 in order that in the coming ages he might show *the incomparable riches of his grace,* expressed in his kindness to us in Christ Jesus.

God's grace is exceedingly abundant and can be lavished on us if we are open to it.

Ro 5:17 For if, by the trespass of the one man, death reigned through that one man, *how much more will those who receive God's abundant provision of grace and of the gift of righteousness reign in life through the one man, Jesus Christ.*

2Co 9:14 And in their prayers for you their hearts will go out to you, because of the *surpassing grace God has given you.*

Eph 1:4 For he chose us in him before the creation of the world to be holy and blameless in his sight. In love

Eph 1:5 he predestined us to be adopted as his sons [become true children of God] through Jesus Christ, in accordance with his pleasure and will—

Eph 1:6 *to the praise of his glorious grace*, which he has freely given us in the One he loves [Jesus].

Eph 1:7 In him we have redemption ..., the forgiveness of sins, *in accordance with the riches of God's grace*

Eph 1:8 that he lavished on us with all wisdom and understanding.

Eph 2:7 in order that in the coming ages he might show *the incomparable riches of his grace*, expressed in his kindness to us in Christ Jesus.

1Ti 1:14 The *grace of our Lord was poured out on me abundantly*, along with the faith and love that are in Christ Jesus.

2Pe 1:2 *Grace and peace be yours in abundance through the knowledge of God and of Jesus our Lord.* (Also 1 Pe 1:2)

How Is Grace Connected to the Kingdom?

Paul equates the gospel of grace to preaching the kingdom. There are 150 references to the kingdom in the New Testament and the majority are either Kingdom of God (65 times throughout the gospels and epistles) and Kingdom of heaven (31 times, in the gospel of Matthew only).

There is no difference between these two expressions — they both refer to the realm of the saved. Jesus came to bring the gospel (good news) of the Kingdom of God/Heaven and taught how one could enter this Kingdom – become a saved and redeemed child of God. Jesus brought immortality and salvation to light:

2Tim 1:9-10 [God] has saved us and called us to a holy life—*not because of anything we have done but because of his own purpose and grace. This grace was given us in Christ Jesus* before the beginning of time, but it has now been revealed through the appearing of our Savior, Christ

Jesus, who has destroyed death and has *brought life and immortality to light through the gospel.*

So salvation – entering/seeing the Kingdom is by grace. It is not dependent on anything that we have done and is not earned or deserved by us.

Jesus also told Nicodemus that the condition for seeing the Kingdom was to be born again (John 3:3). He also spoke of the Holy Spirit, which Paul in Romans 5:5 tells us brings God's Love into our hearts.

Jesus was the first to possess God's Divine Love and commanded his disciples to love one another as he loved them (John 13:34, 15:12), i.e., with the Divine Love, which transcends our natural human love that we are born with.

Jesus is the firstborn of many siblings (Rom. 8:29), and the first to have entered the Kingdom of God/Kingdom of heaven where he is the head or master (Col. 1:18). The church can be seen as "the Kingdom of God in embryo" — those still on earth who are following in Jesus' footsteps as his younger brothers and sisters.

The new birth/salvation means to have one's soul transformed by the Divine Love from the image of God into the substance of God and to become at one with God through fully acquiring His divine nature. (2 Pet. 1:4). Those so transformed become God's true and redeemed children who can enter the Kingdom of God.

Quoting from *True Gospel Revealed Anew by Jesus*, Vol. 3, p. 43:

"I meant that in the Kingdom of God there are homes and that I would go and prepare a place where my followers should have a home with me, separate from the homes of the spirits who are not believers in or followers of me; that my kingdom was to be a separate kingdom from the other parts of the spirit lands, and *that those who wanted to live with me would have to get this love of God in their hearts to do so. My kingdom is one where Love is supreme and where it is manifested in the purest and highest degree.* I have not seen God in the sense that I have seen you, but that in the sense that my love is so very abundant and so truly His Love, that He appears to my soul's eyes just as plainly as you appear to my natural eyes.

Many of my sayings were merely symbolical and not intended to be taken literally. My Father cannot be seen by anyone of His children, and no man has ever seen Him, for He is not of form or substance that can be seen. *You are now very near where you will see Him with your soul's eyes, as I did, and when you do, then you will be able to know that His Love is in your heart to its fullest.* Why you are so greatly blessed with this Love and faith I really do not know, even though I do know so much of His truth and Love. But I see that you have great possibilities of faith and love which will make you a most wonderful man doing His work of saving souls for His kingdom."

All this happens by grace – everything for our salvation can be given to us freely by God and is available for the asking through sincere heartfelt prayer. All we need to do is graciously accept these gifts and work on increasing them in our lives – grow in the divine nature and in God's Love so that we will reach the point of full soul transformation into sinless divine beings – a totally new creation (2 Cor 5:17).

How Is the Gospel of Grace the Full Will of God

The gospel is an all-encompassing plan of God to fulfill his purpose for humanity – His highest created beings on earth that at the beginning made a very wrong choice and since then have largely been going astray and becoming "dead in sins" (Eph. 2:1-5). God's plan is to save people from their sins, bring them back from death to spiritual life and help them to become transformed through His Love and divine nature.

Eph 2:1-5 As for you, you were dead in your transgressions and sins, in which you used to live when you followed the ways of this world ... gratifying the cravings of [your] sinful nature and following its desires and thoughts. ... But because of his great love for us, God, who is rich in mercy, made us alive with Christ even when we were dead in transgressions—it is by grace you have been saved.

Other than the gospel of God's grace (Acts 20:24) and the gospel of the kingdom (Matt. 24:14), the message of salvation that Jesus brought is referred to as gospel about Jesus Christ (Mark 1:1); gospel of Christ (Rom. 15:19 and seven other references); gospel of the glory of Christ (2 Cor 4:4); gospel of God's son (Rom 1:9); gospel of our Lord Jesus (2 Thess. 1:8); gospel of God (Rom. 15:16 and five other references); gospel of the blessed God (1 Tim 1:11); gospel of your salvation (Eph. 1:13); gospel of peace (Eph. 1:13). Each of these could be elaborated on further.

In a nutshell, Jesus, who from birth was spiritually inclined, was commissioned by God to preach the good news of salvation – the rebestowal of God's Love that was withheld after the first humans rejected it. Jesus recognized the presence of this Love in himself and correctly perceived that this was the fulfillment of the Old Testament prophecies of the new heart (Eze 36:26; Jer. 24:7). His experience, teaching and example of God's Love in his life is the key to the fulfillment of God's purpose and His ultimate will for humanity.

How can we avail ourselves of God's offer of abundant grace that will place us on the path to salvation and an incredible future in God's Celestial Kingdom for all eternity?

As mentioned, God's gifts of grace are free for the asking. God wants us to have a relationship with Him, not just as His created children (which we all already are), but as His true redeemed children who are becoming at one with Him and share more and more in His Divine Love and nature. To start on the journey to this special relationship, simply express your love and desire to get to know God as your loving heavenly Father and to have Him in your life. Ask Him to open your soul to the inflowing of His Love imparted by the Holy Spirit (Rom. 5:5) to transform you. Build a daily prayer habit and maintain an ongoing relationship with God, asking for guidance, mercy and His Love as often as you can.

As time goes on, you'll notice a self-transformation. Your desires will change and become more spiritually oriented. Things and values of the world will become of less and less interest and importance. You'll become more kind and loving. More peace will be yours. You may also feel sensations in your heart region which is connected with or a doorway to the soul. You may become aware of spiritual gifts to serve others. All this and other positive changes are evidence of you becoming a new creature/creation (2 Cor 5:17), of having a heart change (spiritual heart transplant if you will), of moving toward the new birth that Jesus talked to Nicodemus about (John 3:3). It is a process that in due time will culminate in a full transformation into a divine being and a place in the Kingdom of God with never-ending opportunities for further growth in love, joy and closeness to your heavenly Father.

Paul's Experience of God's Saving Grace

This chapter, spinning from two messages received by James Padgett in 1915, deals with three lessons from the Apostle Paul's spiritual life.

Just over a year after Jesus started working with James Padgett and communicating spiritual messages through him, in December 1915, Jesus spoke about the apostle Paul and his dramatic conversion and calling based on a speaker's interpretation of the Bible account in Acts 9. Quoting from *True Gospel Revealed Anew by Jesus,* Vol. 2, p. 377 (emphasis mine):

"... the whole discourse was taken from the Bible, and ... [the speaker's description of Paul's experience on the way to Damascus] is partly true, and partly not. ... When he was felled to the ground by the brightness of the great light that shone about him, Paul heard what I said, and answered me, and went into the town; but he was not blind, nor did the prophet Ananias do anything to him in the way of curing any physical blindness; *he only helped to open the spiritual blindness of Paul, and show him the way to the Father's Love and Kingdom.*

"Paul, as you know, was a very learned man among the Jews, and was a strict believer and follower of the

Pharisees' doctrines; but as to knowing anything about the Divine Love, he had never experienced it, nor even did know what it was intellectually. *My summons to him was not only for the purpose of stopping the persecution of my people, but for the further purpose of enlisting him in my cause,* as not many of my followers were educated or learned men, and I realized that my doctrines and truths must be preached among not only the learned Jews, but also among the gentile philosophers; and as the first requisite in such cases is to hold and, in a way, convince the intellect, *I saw that I must have a disciple who would have the mental qualifications to present to these learned men, in a convincing way, my truths, and be able to withstand the logic and reasoning of these gentile philosophers.*

"John was filled with Love, and wherever he could come in close communion with the common people, *he could, by the great power and influence of that Love, persuade these people to embrace and receive my truths,* and as a consequence, feel the inflowing of the Holy Spirit. But Paul had not this Love to that degree, as to be enabled by virtue of its power or influence to convince and compel his hearers to receive my truths, and embrace that faith in my teachings as would cause them to seek the Love of the Father; and hence, *his mission was the more intended to be the teachings of my truths to the intellect and mental perceptions of a large number of persons of greater intellectual development than those with whom John and the other disciples would come in contact."*

"[Paul] ... became a wonderful power in spreading my truths, and in convincing men that the Love of the Father was the one great possession to be obtained, and in causing them to believe in me as the son of the Father, and His messenger to declare to the world the great plan of man's salvation.

"Paul finally became a man filled with this Love *as far as his nature was capable of receiving it,* and in his gospel will be found wonderful exhortations to his hearers to seek for it. *But he was not the disciple of Love, but rather of the intellectual parts of my truths; and when he taught, his teachings were intended to appeal more to the mental perceptions, than to the soul perceptions.*"

In a follow-on message, *True Gospel Revealed Anew by Jesus,* Vol. 2, p. 379, Paul himself comments: "... *my only blindness was that which covered my spiritual eyes* at the time. And, when I went into the town, *the only blindness that I recovered from, in a way, was that which had kept my soul in darkness* and caused me to persecute the followers of Jesus under the belief that I was doing the work which God had called me to do. ... *I was more of an intellectual Christian in my early ministry than a Christian possessing the Great Divine Love of the Father.* Yet, thanks to him, I continued to preach and believed as best I could until, finally, I became a redeemed child of God, filled with His Love."

At least three concepts in these two accounts bear commenting on. They are God's calling, healing of spiritual blindness, and an intellectual versus a soul approach.

God's Calling

While God gives each and every one of us a free choice whether or not to accept His truth and/or gift of Divine Love, I believe that we each also receive a calling. The above message uses even a stronger word, namely "summons". Jesus' *summons* to Paul was not only for him to stop organized persecution of Christians but also to be *enlisted* (another interesting word in this context) in Jesus' cause.

The Bible uses the same word in an encouraging context in the Book of Isaiah, speaking in a national context to Israel, but the same would apply individually to each of God's children. Isaiah 43:1 – "But now, this is what the LORD says—*he who created you* [created your soul], ... he who *formed you* [formed your body in the womb] ...: "Fear not, for I have *redeemed you*; *I have summoned you by name*; you are mine [my created child with the potential to become my true child through the transformation by my Love]."

And again in Isaiah 45:3 – "I will give you the *treasures* of darkness, *riches* stored in secret places [hidden treasures of the Celestial Kingdom that need to be discovered – see Matthew 13:44], so that you may know that I am the LORD, the God of Israel, who *summons you by name*."

And once more in Isaiah 49:1 – "*Before I was born the LORD called me* [when I was just an un-incarnated soul]; from my birth he has made mention of my name."

One could say, we are not Isaiah, the apostle Paul, or James Padgett, who all had an obvious function and purpose in God's plan. That is true, but we all have God-given gifts and a purpose in God's plan of salvation. The New Testament talks about a calling in numerous places, but I'll just quote Romans 8:28, which speaks collectively and is very encouraging: "And we know that in all things God works for the good of those who love him, who *have been called according to his purpose*."

The question may arise, if we are called (or even summoned) by God, where is free choice? It is still there as we can reject, refuse and/or resist our calling. But of course, the law of cause and effect will apply, and worse still, we would be rejecting a wonderful privilege, reward and future. So once we are given spiritual understanding and our eyes are open to this, we would much less likely want to reject our calling. And that brings us to the next point ...

Healing of Spiritual Blindness

Regarding Paul's calling, or to use Jesus' word, "summons", which was more dramatic than most of us might experience, Jesus says: "[Ananias] *only helped to open the spiritual blindness of Paul, and show him the way to the Father's Love and Kingdom.*" Paul himself elaborates: "... *my only blindness was that which covered my spiritual eyes* at the time. And, when I went into the town, *the only blindness that I recovered from, in a way, was that which had kept my soul in darkness.*"

The Bible uses healing from blindness in several meanings, ranging from a one-of opening eyes to physical or spiritual realities, healing those who were physically blind, and revealing spiritual truths to which many are blind by virtue of ingrained beliefs, acquired prejudices, being too steeped in the material world, or other factors. Further healing of spiritual blindness at a deeper level involves opening of soul perceptions which happens as Divine Love begins transforming the soul.

In Paul's case, his eyes were opened to see what kept his soul in darkness and to see the way to God's Kingdom through the Father's Love. In recounting his Damascus road experience to King Agrippa in the book of Acts, Paul explains the commission that Jesus subsequently gave him: Acts 26:17-18 – "... I am sending you to them [the gentiles or non-Jews] *to open their eyes and turn them from darkness to light,* and from the power of Satan to God, so that they may receive forgiveness of sins and a place among those who are sanctified by faith in me."

This can also be seen as our calling and commission – *to open people's eyes and turn them from darkness to light,* which if they then follow the path of light will lead them to forgiveness and a place in God's Celestial Kingdom.

How can this be done? There are various ways, according to our individual gifts and guidance. As the above message says, John did it through the abundance of God's Love in his soul. Paul did it through intellectual teaching and reasoning. One could say that John was very much of a "soul person" whereas Paul was a lot more of the mind and intellect. Was one a better servant of God, or spiritually superior than the other? Sometimes, we may get the impression that those among us who are more soul-oriented are better or better off. But let's continue ...

Intellectual/Mind versus Soul/Heart Approach

The above message clearly shows that both the "soul people" and the "mind people" are needed to carry out God's plan. That's because the world has both types and multitude of shades in between them. We are all unique in this and other respects, and God has need and use for each and every one of us who has had their eyes open to understand spiritual truths and has accepted His calling to help bring about His plan of salvation.

In the time of the early church, Jesus needed *"a disciple who would have the mental qualifications to present to these learned men, in a convincing way, [his] truths, and be able to withstand the logic and reasoning of these gentile philosophers. ... [Paul's] mission was more intended to be the teachings of my truths to the intellect and mental perceptions of a large number of persons of greater intellectual development.... His teachings were intended to appeal more to the mental perceptions, than to the soul perceptions."*

With the Western world in particular being largely mind-oriented, it too no doubt needs those who can meet people where they are in this way. Those among us who are more intellectual are just as needed as those who operate more from the soul. The key is not so much mind/intellect versus soul. Rather it is that the mind, intellect and soul are all on a spiritual wavelength and working together. Time after time, in order to get into spiritual condition sufficient to make rapport with the angels, James Padgett was exhorted to think spiritual thoughts and to pray more. That would then result in soul longings and more Divine Love in the soul, which would lead to increased soul development.

In conclusion, whether we are more like John or more like Paul or anywhere in between, let's all accept ourselves and one another, work together, use our gifts, support and encourage each other, and look forward to our indescribably beautiful, happy and glorious future in God's Celestial Kingdom.

False and True Grace

Christian churches emphasize moral and ethical living largely based on the Ten Commandments. They also teach about "grace" through Jesus' sacrifice for sin by dying on the cross. Members are taught that if they repent and believe that Jesus paid the penalty for their sins, they are reconciled with God.

While they may believe in Jesus' sacrifice and vicarious atonement, Christians are still subject to temptations and continue to sin. Sincere church members strive to overcome their back-sliding nature, often becoming discouraged or frustrated at the lack of progress. Others strive less and maintain a false sense of security in their belief that they are saved as a result of their faith in Jesus. Because of this scenario, Christianity can degenerate into a religion where a person may continue to violate God's laws (in that Jesus' blood will "cover" the sins of those who believe in his name), and wherein God can accept into His holy house a sin-laden soul merely because of faith in Jesus. Alternatively, it remains a religion not unlike Judaism, with the reliance on law obedience for the purpose of soul purification and as a "way" to God. There is no transformation of the soul – only purification, and therefore no fulfilment of the law by grace.

The truth is that the above is not the grace that Jesus taught and indeed is not grace at all. Neither Jesus' nor anyone else's blood has to power to wash away our sins. Also, a soul is naturally purified only to the extent that it is obedient to God's laws.

The message of grace that Jesus taught, and that is contained in the Bible but significantly downplayed and almost unnoticed, is that humans can pray for and obtain God's Divine Love. This gift of love imparted by the Holy Spirit into the soul can progressively transform the human soul into an immortal divine soul. It is what the Old Testament prophets referred to as the "new heart", which empowers change and enables the recipient of the Divine Love to more and more avoid sin.

The Divine Love is the real grace which ultimately eliminates sin from the soul as it affects its transformation into a divine soul, and thus brings about a soul condition whereby the laws of Moses are no longer needed. The law is fulfilled by the divine presence of the Father Himself through the Divine Love in the souls of those to whom it comes in response to earnest prayer. It is this love that is the fulfilment of the law.

With the false teaching of grace through the sacrifice and vicarious atonement of Jesus, many do not know about and so do not ask for the Divine Love and are therefore left to their own resources for overcoming sin. Yet, the Father is more than happy to impart the gift of His Love into the souls of those who pray to Him in sincerity and truth. The resultant transformation of the human soul into a divine soul is the true grace and fulfilment of the law.

For more details about the two different "gospels" – one of which is truly a gospel of grace while the other one provides a false sense of security, see "Reflection on the Gospels" on the next page.

Reflection on the Gospels

Jesus was born as the prophesied Messiah or anointed one. While the Jews expected a Messiah's coming based on ancient prophecies, they were hoping for a conqueror who would free Judea from Roman domination and set up an earthly kingdom. While Jesus came as a king, his kingdom was not of this world. Rather, it was the kingdom of God – a Celestial Kingdom of Divine Love.

The anointing that Jesus received involved having in his heart and soul the presence of the Divine Love imparted by the Holy Spirit. This was a gift from God given first to Jesus, but thereafter available to all who would ask for it with sincere and heartfelt prayer. Thus Jesus was the first of many brethren to become a true child of God (Romans 8:29), whose soul became transformed by the Divine Love from divine image to divine substance.

The message of the Divine Love that Jesus brought became lost in the copying and rewriting of the original biblical texts, but traces of it can be seen throughout, in the same way that other traces of the early Christian teachings are apparent.

Indeed, the New Testament gospels contain several intertwining messages. This is the result of historical events being perceived and recorded by various individuals, as well as follow-up reinterpretations and editing by later writers and editors whose thinking and prejudices found their way into the texts as well. This article addresses two of the threads – namely the message of Jesus versus a later message about Jesus.

Jesus' Teaching

Key thoughts of the message that Jesus brought deal with the availability of Divine Love (imparted by the Holy Spirit) as follows:

1. God is love (1 John 4:8, 16). This love transcends the natural human love, which at its best can include unconditional acceptance and lofty deeds.

2. God's love was displayed by sending Jesus (1 John 4:9) and through him the message that the Divine Love and nature is available to humans as a gift for the asking. This was also the message that God's kingdom was near (Matt. 4:17). Through acquiring the Divine Love, by which the individual will would align with divine will, the way to God's kingdom (the Celestial Spheres) was open (Matt. 7:21).

3. Jesus, as the Messiah (Christ or anointed) was the first to experience the new birth that he taught about. He manifested the Divine Love, received through the Holy Spirit, and set an example of a life motivated by this love (Matt. 11:29). While his countrymen expected him to establish an earthly kingdom and overthrow the Romans, Jesus taught that his kingdom was not visible in the ordinary sense. Yet, the kingdom was *among them* – through his person, and could

be *within them* – by receiving the Divine Love in their souls as he had (Luke 17:21 – the Greek word can have both meanings).

4. Those who in their soul desire the gift of the Divine Love and sincerely pray for it will receive it and have their soul transformed from divine image into divine substance. This is the new birth – being born again of imperishable seed or being born of God (John 1:13; 3:3, 5; Titus 3:5; 1 Peter 1:23; 1 John 4:7).

5. Jesus practiced and taught love for one another (1 John 3:11). The apostle John, who among the disciples was spiritually the closest to Jesus, later showed how if we truly love one another and walk as Jesus did, God lives in us and we in Him, and His love is made complete in us (1 John 2:5-6; 4:12, 16). The Divine Love transforming our souls gives us the knowledge of our unity with the Father (John 7:20-26).

6. The Holy Spirit is a spirit of power, love and self-control (Acts 1:8; 2 Tim. 1:7). Jesus and his disciples manifested the gift of the Divine Love by the power to heal (e.g. Matt. 4:23; 12:15; 14:14).

7. Jesus also used parables to help people understand the preciousness of this powerful, yet invisible gift, comparing it to a treasure or a pearl of great value worth all that one has (Matt. 13:44-46). He also showed its power to transform through the parables of the mustard seed and yeast in a batch of dough (Matt. 13:31-32). He taught that the Father is more willing to

grant this gift to His children than earthly parents enjoy giving good gifts to their offspring (Luke 11:13).

8. The gift of the Divine Love is referred to in the New Testament as

- Gift of grace (2 Cor. 9:15)
- Salvation by grace (not because of good deeds), through the washing of rebirth /new birth and renewal by the Holy Spirit (Tit. 3:5)
- Participation in the divine nature (2 Pet. 1:4)
- God's glory (in the form of divine nature); it unites those who possess it and through their lives makes God known to those who don't (John 17:20-26)
- Experiencing the fullness of God (Eph. 3:19)
- Power that works in us (Eph. 3:20)
- Power of God for salvation and righteousness of God by faith (Rom. 1:16-17)
- God's light shining in our hearts to give us the knowledge of the glory of God (2 Cor. 4:6)
- Source of life and immortality (2 Tim. 1:10)
- Love poured into our hearts by the Holy Spirit (Rom. 5:5)
- Love that surpasses all other gifts as well as knowledge (1 Cor. 13:1-3; Eph. 3:18-19)
- Being rooted and established in love (Eph. 3:17)
- Gift of the Holy Spirit, the spirit of grace (Luke 11:13; Acts 10:45, Heb. 10:29)

- Streams of living waters — the received Holy Spirit (John 7:38-39; 20:22) Note: God is metaphorically called the spring of living water (Jer. 2:13, 17:13)
- Living water permanently quenching [spiritual] thirst and becoming a spring welling up to eternal life (John 4:10-14).
- Spirit in our inner being (heart or soul) (Eph. 3:16; 2 Tim. 1:14), motivating us to do what is right (Rom. 7:22)
- Spirit of love and other God-like qualities that transcend the law (Gal. 5:22-23)
- Spirit in our hearts as a deposit for our glorious future in God's kingdom (2 Cor. 1:22)
- Spirit which makes us true children of the Father and at one with Him, as well as heirs of divine glory (Rom. 8:9, 14-17)
- Anointing (1 John 2:20-27; 2 Cor. 1:21)
- Christ (the anointing that came with Jesus) dwelling in our hearts through faith (Eph. 3:17)
- Christ in us, the hope of glory (Col. 1:27)
- Being in Christ and becoming a new creation (2 Cor. 5:17; Gal. 6:15)
- Conversion through having the door of faith opened by God (Acts 14:27; 15:3)
- Being transformed and made new by the renewing of the mind (Rom 12:2; Eph. 4:23)

- Putting on the new self to be like God in righteousness and holiness (Eph. 4:24)
- Walking in the Spirit (Gal. 5:16, 25)
- Loving one another as a result of God-given love, through which we know God and are born of God (1 John 4:7-8)

In addition to the above, many biblical references to the Holy Spirit can be seen as synonymous with Divine Love in that the Spirit, as the Divine Love, is a means of conversion, new life, new heart, becoming a new creation / creature, salvation, and resurrection to immortality.

Another "Gospel"

In addition to the message about the Divine Love that Jesus preached and exemplified, the gospel books and other New Testament writings also contain a second "gospel" – about Jesus and emphasizing his death by crucifixion which paid the penalty for our sins. In contrast to Jesus' own message, this one was introduced by others who subsequently tried to make sense of and explain the "impermissible" death of the Messiah.

Jesus as the Messiah was expected to overthrow the Romans, not be killed by them – despite the fact that Jesus stressed that his kingdom was not of this world (John 18:36). His unexpected death then became interpreted as a part of God's plan in providing a sacrifice for sin and a vicarious atonement.

In keeping with the interpretation of Jesus' death, authors and editors of New Testament books reframed the narratives of his life to conform to these ideas. Words were placed in Jesus' mouth and Hebrew Scriptures misquoted or quoted out of context to substantiate the concept of Jesus as a "sacrificial lamb" paralleling the lambs killed at Passover whose blood applied to doorposts saved the Israelite firstborn from death at the time of the Exodus (Ex. 12).

It is true that Jesus fulfilled some Old Testament prophecies, but care is needed in determining what passages apply to him and which ones do not. It is true that Jesus died at Passover at the same time that the Passover lambs were being killed for the traditional Passover meal. But does that automatically make him the fulfillment of what the original Passover signified? Is the story of the Passover and the Ten Plagues on Egypt based in fact or is it symbolic or allegorical? How much of it is literally true? It is beyond the scope here to delve into details, but suffice it to say that the Pentateuch books (Gen.-Deut.) and much of the Old Testament were compiled retrospectively by scribes like Ezra during and after the Babylonian exile. There seems to be little or no conclusive evidence from Egyptian records or archaeology for the story of the Plagues and the Exodus.

In addition to the above uncertainty, there is a logistical conflict between the two messages or "gospels". On the one hand, God's love and salvation is a gift from a loving and merciful Father, while on the other hand, the gift first had to be paid for as a ransom to satisfy a wrathful God. These ideas are also incompatible in that Jesus (as supposed God) would have had to pay for his own gift with his life or pay for the Father's gift – in which case it would have been a gift from Jesus, not the Father. Yet Jesus teaches that the gift of salvation is given by God (John 4:10). In addition, God owns everything and can bestow gifts and absolve debts (Luke 15:21-24) – without requiring a sacrifice.

We also get the impression that while Jesus travelled from town to town preaching, his message always dealt with present matters, not with his future death as a payment for sin. Rather the kingdom of God and the new birth were available in the present (John 3:1-8; Luke 4:21). Therefore the often quoted verse of John 3:16 stating that "God so loved the world that he gave his one and only Son, that whoever believes in him shall not perish but have eternal life" would read better as "God so loved the world that he gave us *his divine love, that whoever receives it* shall not perish but have eternal life."

In summary, there is no efficacy in Jesus' blood to save or pay for human sins and reconcile people to the Father. The New Testament does not even conclusively prove that Jesus is God – that idea was decided by 4th century

Councils of bishops after much discussion. That being the case, those who believe in Jesus' death as a means of their salvation may be under a false sense of security. They may also be neglecting the one vital requirement for salvation, and that is the new birth (John 3:3). This and this only saves humans from their sins and fits them to enter the Celestial Kingdom of God, which is the kingdom of Jesus, for he is the Prince of that kingdom, and the master and ruler thereof.

The next chapter briefly explains what is the new birth that, as Jesus told Nicodemus (John 3), is the necessary prerequisite for salvation in the Kingdom of God.

PART III – NEW BIRTH: ITS ASPECTS

New Birth

Jesus told to Nicodemus when asked regarding entering the Kingdom of God: *"You must be born again"*. What was this new birth that he was talking about?

The following biblical terms (based on the NIV version) are interchangeable and mean the same thing – the Celestial Kingdom of God: Kingdom of Heaven (used almost exclusively in the gospel of Matthew); Kingdom of God (the most common expression used 65 times in the gospels, book of Acts, and some of Paul's letters); and my [Jesus'] Father's Kingdom (used once in Matthew 26:29).

"Being born again", which has also been translated as "born from above" has the following equivalents, all referring to the new birth (1 Pet 1:23): born of God (John 1:13); and born of the spirit (John 3:6-8).

So those who wish to enter the Celestial Kingdom (be saved) must first undergo the new birth. What does that mean?

Salvation and redemption means becoming at one, or achieve at-onement, with God. This cannot be achieved through faith in Jesus' sacrifice on the cross or even just human overcoming of sin. (Jesus' sacrifice can do nothing as far as transformation of individual souls.) The only way

New Birth

a person can achieve unity with God is through being born again or anew (John 1:13; 3:1-8) whereby the Holy Spirit imparts the Love of God into their heart (Rom. 5:5) and transforms their soul from being in the image of God to acquiring divine substance.

Without the Divine Love, humans are neither divine nor have God living in them. They are only created in the image of God, not possessing the substance of God. This too applies only at the soul level, not the body level, for God does not possess a body in human shape. The new birth means that the soul, made in the image of God, is by the Divine Love transformed into the substance of God. The Bible also refers to the result of this process as becoming a new creature / creation; being born again or born of God; and rebirth and renewal by the Holy Spirit (John 1:13; 2 Cor. 5:17; Gal. 6:15; 1 Pet. 1:23; Titus 3:5; 1 John 3:9 and 4:7).

Through the new birth, humans become at one with the Father. This is the effect of the Divine Love flowing into one's soul and replacing all that tends to sin and error. As the Divine Love takes over the soul, it changes it to the quality of the Great Soul of the Father. Thus the human becomes divine and immortal with their soul not only in the image of God, but also of divine substance. This, upon death and passing into the spirit world, enables them to progress and eventually enter the Celestial Kingdom of God.

New Birth

The soul transformation leading to the new birth also spiritually achieves a number of things, which will be explored in the next few chapters. These are:

- God living in us and we in Him
- Oneness with the Father
- Christ in us

We'll also briefly explore the work of the Holy Spirit / spirit of truth / Counsellor.

God in Us and We in Him

John, in his gospel, is quoting Jesus on several occasions as follows:

Jn 10:37-38 Do not believe me unless I do what my Father does. But if I do it, even though you do not believe me, believe the miracles, that you may know and understand that *the Father is in me, and I in the Father."*

Jn 14:10-11 Don't you believe that *I am in the Father, and that the Father is in me*? The words I say to you are not just my own. Rather, *it is the Father, living in me, who is doing his work.* Believe me when I say that *I am in the Father and the Father is in me*; or at least believe on the evidence of the miracles themselves.

Jn 14:15 "If you love me, you will obey what I command.

Jn 14:16 And I will ask the Father, and he will give you another Counselor to be with you forever—

Jn 14:17 the *Spirit of truth. The world cannot accept him, because it neither sees him nor knows him. But you know him, for he lives with you and will be in you.*

Jn 14:18 *I will not leave you as orphans; I will come to you.*

Jn 14:19 Before long, the world will not see me anymore, but *you will see me. Because I live, you also will live.*

Jn 14:20 *On that day you will realize that I am in my Father, and you are in me, and I am in you.*

Jn 14:21 Whoever has my commands and obeys them, he is the one who loves me. He who loves me will be loved by my Father, and I too will love him and show myself to him." ...

Jn 14:23 Jesus replied, *"If anyone loves me, he will obey my teaching. My Father will love him, and we will come to him and make our home with him.* ...

Jn 14:26 But the *Counselor, the Holy Spirit, whom the Father will send in my name, will teach you all things and will remind you of everything I have said to you.*

Jn 14:27 Peace I leave with you; my peace I give you. I do not give to you as the world gives. Do not let your hearts be troubled and do not be afraid.

Jn 15:5 "I am the vine; you are the branches. *If a man remains in me and I in him, he will bear much fruit;* ...

Jn 15:8 This is to my Father's glory, that you bear much fruit, showing yourselves to be my disciples.

Jn 15:9 *"As the Father has loved me, so have I loved you. Now remain in my love.*

Jn 15:10 *If you obey my commands, you will remain in my love, just as I have obeyed my Father's commands and remain in his love.* ...

Jn 15:12 *My command is this: Love each other as I have loved you* [with God's Divine Love]. ...

Jn 15:15 I no longer call you servants, because a servant does not know his master's business. Instead, I have called you friends, for *everything that I learned from my Father I have made known to you* [Jesus brought life and immortality and salvation through the Divine Love to light through his teachings – 2 Tim 1:10].

Jn 17:11 I will remain in the world no longer, but they are still in the world, and I am coming to you. *Holy Father, protect them by the power of your name—the name you gave me—so that they may be one as we are one.* ...

Jn 17:20 "My prayer is not for them alone. *I pray also for those who will believe in me through their message,*
Jn 17:21 that all of them may be one, Father, just as you are in me and I am in you. May they also be in us so that the world may believe that you have sent me.
Jn 17:22 I have given them the glory that you gave me, that they may be one as we are one:
Jn 17:23 I in them and you in me. May they be brought to complete unity to let the world know that you sent me and have loved them even as you have loved me. ...

Jn 17:26 *I have made you known to them, and will continue to make you known in order that the love you have for me may be in them and that I myself may be in them.*"

Let's bring these ideas together to get an overview and a better understanding:

- The Father is in me [Jesus], and I in the Father (mentioned three times).
- It is the Father, living in Jesus, who is doing His work.
- Jesus commanded his disciples to love him as he loved them – with the Divine Love that was in his heart. This was the key to the oneness, connection and mutual love between God, Jesus and the disciples.
- If we live in Jesus and he in us, we'll bear much fruit, whereby the Father will be glorified.
- The Father will give Jesus' disciples another Counselor forever— the Spirit of truth. … he will be in them.
- I [Jesus] will come to you. … Because I live, you also will live. … you will realize that I am in my Father, and you are in me, and I am in you.
- Jesus prayed that the disciples may be one as he and the Father were one.
- He also prayed for future disciples – those "who will believe in me through their message, that all of them may be one, Father, just as you are in me and I am in you".
- I have given them the glory that you gave me, that they may be one as we are one: I in them and you in me. May they be brought to complete unity to let the world know that you sent me and have loved them even as you have loved me. …
- I have made you known to them, and will continue to make you known in order that the love you have for me may be in them and that I myself may be in them.

So while we are still individuals and will always retain our unique personalities, we can become a part of and at one with God – living in Him and Him in us. We can be in the same relationship with Jesus and each other as Jesus' disciples. How does this unity or at-oness occur?

Becoming At-One with Father

The key to oneness with our Heavenly Father is acquiring His Love/Substance imparted by the Holy Spirit (Rom. 5:5) and being transformed by it at the soul level. The below extra-biblical messages elaborate further.

This message from Jesus found in *53 New Testament Revelations*, Rev. 5, says this: "I further stated that *even as the Father knew and was in me through having bestowed upon me the gift of His Love through response to my soul aspirations and prayer, and this Love was His nature and essence, even so did I know the Father and in the same way was in Him.*"

Jesus further comments in *53 New Testament Revelations*, Rev.23: "I also said, 'If a man love me he will observe my message; if ye keep my commandment ye shall abide in my love, even as I have kept my Father's commandments and abide in His Love,' which was another way of saying that *those disciples who believed I was the Messiah and loved me would believe that my soul was an immortal one through the Divine Love and pray to the Father for His Love as the way to at-onement with Him and immortality,* which was the message I taught and which I asked my disciples, and all my hearers, to apply to themselves and actually pray, and the result would be that *they would be filled with the same Love as I was and that we could thus have a mutual Love for one another in the same way* that as I prayed to the Father and received more of His Love, I loved God more and more, and His Love for me was in my heart."

And again, quoting from *True Gospel Revealed Anew by Jesus*, Vol. 2, p.322: "Yet [Jesus] became more than the perfect man, and *it was only after he attained to this condition of excellence, that he could say, "I and my Father are one," for it was then only that he possessed the Divine Love to that degree which made him at-one with the Father. Only he is at-one with the Father that realizes that he is possessed of the very nature and Essence of the Father*, and there is only one way in which this can be obtained, and that is by the inflowing into the soul of the Divine Love. Jesus could not say to the multitude that they were at-one with him and with the Father, for they had only the natural love and had not experienced the transformation of their souls; and such sayings as this were addressed only to his disciples, or to those among his hearers that had received this Love."

And one more reference – *True Gospel Revealed Anew by Jesus*, Vol 3, p. 328: "Only the inflowing of this Love can reconcile men with God in the higher and desirable sense. Of course they may become in harmony with Him by a purification of their natural love, but that is the harmony only that existed between Him and the first parents before their fall, and is not the harmony which Jesus taught and which was the object of his mission to teach. *When he said "I and my Father are one", he did not refer to the atonement between the mere image and the substance, but to the at-onement which gives to the souls of men the very substance of Father."*

In summary, there is a oneness and intimate closeness between Jesus and the Father. This is because while on earth, since childhood, Jesus was partaking of the Father's Love and substance which fully transformed his soul enabling him to experience the new heart and new birth. The same oneness and intimacy is available to Jesus' disciples. We too can each experience it through our souls being transformed by God's Divine Love, which is free for the asking. When sufficient transformation occurs, we are in the Father and the Father is in us and also Jesus is in us. This soul transformation enables Jesus and his disciples to do great works – bear fruit, by which the Father is glorified.

The next chapter explores the concept of "Christ in us".

Christ in Us

Jesus said that he would come to live in us which would enable us to experience the same connection and closeness he has with the Father (John 14:18-20). Paul elaborated on this idea of "Christ in us" in several of his epistles.

"Christ" is a title and means "anointed one". Jesus became the Christ only because he was the first to receive the Divine Love into his soul and manifest its existence. He was also the first to preach this message of Divine Love and the Holy Spirit (Rom. 5:5). It was his gospel of the Kingdom (Matt. 24:14), also referred to as the gospel of grace (Acts 20:24), gospel about Jesus Christ (Mark 1:1); gospel of Christ (Rom. 15:19); gospel of the glory of Christ (2 Cor 4:4); gospel of God's son (Rom 1:9); gospel of our Lord Jesus (2 Thess. 1:8); gospel of God / the blessed God (Rom. 15:16, 1 Tim 1:11); and gospel of your salvation and of peace (Eph. 1:13).

The Divine Love or *Christ principle* (anointing) is available to all. The result is that they will become at one with the Father in His substance of Love and immortality. They become saved and redeemed children of God. Jesus is the first-born of many siblings and the one who brought immortality and salvation to light (2 Tim 1:9-10).

The scriptures further express this concept of "Christ in you" as follows:

Col 1:27 To them God has chosen to make known among the Gentiles the *glorious riches of this mystery, which is Christ in you, the hope of glory* [future glorified state in the Celestial Kingdom].

Ro 8:10 But if *Christ is in you*, your body is dead because of sin, yet *your spirit is alive because of righteousness*. ... [This righteousness is obedience to Jesus' teachings – to love one another as he loved his disciples – with the Divine Love: Jn 14:23 Jesus replied, "If anyone loves me, *he will obey my teaching. My Father will love him, and we will come to him and make our home with him.* ...]

2Co 13:5 Examine yourselves to see whether you are in the faith; test yourselves. Do you not realize that *Christ Jesus is in you* — unless, of course, you fail the test? [the self-examination would include obeying Jesus' teaching and "new commandment" (John 13:34).]

Gal 2:20 I have been crucified with Christ [the "old person" symbolically dies] *I no longer live, but Christ lives in me.* The life I live in the body, I live by faith in the Son of God, who loved me ... [a new creation is happening.]

2Co 5:17 Therefore, *if anyone is in Christ, he is a new creation*; the old has gone, the new has come!

To sum up, "Christ in you / us" simply means the anointing that Jesus received through having the Divine Love and substance in his soul. While he was the first, he also brought the message (gospel) that this anointing is available to all for the asking. Once we receive it, we too will have "Christ in us", and be connected to the Father through his own substance and nature – having God in us and being in Him. This is our hope (and guarantee) of glory – becoming glorified divine angels in the Celestial Kingdom of God. Jesus is the first to have entered and is preparing places for those who follow him (John 14:2). He has pre-eminence, being the Master and ruler, and the closest to the fountainhead of God.

The Counsellor / Spirit of Truth / Holy Spirit

Jesus talked about praying for "another Counselor, ... the Spirit of truth," elsewhere also referred to as the Comforter.

Jn 14:16-17 And I will ask the Father, and he will give you another Counselor to be with you forever—the *Spirit of truth*. The world cannot accept him, because it neither sees him nor knows him. But *you know him, for he lives with you and will be in you.*

Jesus, in *53 Revelations*, Rev. 23, explained this as follows. "I simply meant that I would, as I always did, *pray to God so that their souls would be opened up to the Divine Love, which is what the writer meant by the Comforter; and that this Love would continue to be conveyed in more and more abundance into the souls of my disciples throughout all eternity.* I did not mean that I could pray to the Father to send His Divine Love to my disciples merely because of my prayers, but I meant that *the souls of the disciples would have to long for the Father's Love so that it could enter the souls that were in that condition to receive it.*

The coming of the Counsellor / Comforter / spirit of truth / Holy Spirit is also referred to as power and God given glory coming to his disciples. The biblical early church history documented how it happened.

Jn 14:23 Jesus replied, "If anyone loves me, *he will obey my teaching. My Father will love him, and we will come to him and make our home with him.* ...

Jn 14:26 But the *Counselor, the Holy Spirit*, whom the Father will send in my name, *will teach you all things and will remind you of everything I have said to you.*

Ac 2:1 When the day of Pentecost came, they were all together in one place.
Ac 2:2 Suddenly a sound like the blowing of a violent wind came from heaven and filled the whole house where they were sitting.
Ac 2:3 They saw what seemed to be tongues of fire that separated and came to rest on each of them.
Ac 2:4 *All of them were filled with the Holy Spirit* and began to speak in other tongues as the Spirit enabled them.

Ac 2:14 Then Peter stood up with the Eleven, raised his voice and addressed the crowd: "Fellow Jews and all of you who live in Jerusalem, let me explain this to you; listen carefully to what I say.
Ac 2:15 These men are not drunk, as you suppose. It's only nine in the morning!
Ac 2:16 No, this is what was spoken by the prophet Joel:

Ac 2:17 "'In the last days, God says, *I will pour out my Spirit on all people.* [Divine Love will become available to all who desire it.] Your sons and daughters will prophesy, your young men will see visions, your old men will dream dreams.

Ac 2:18 Even on my servants, both men and women, *I will pour out my Spirit in those days*, and they will prophesy [prophecy can mean "inspired teaching"].

Ac 4:31 After they prayed, the place where they were meeting was shaken. And they *were all filled with the Holy Spirit* [received God's Love in abundance] and spoke the word of God boldly.

Ac 4:32 *All the believers were one in heart and mind.* [oneness among the disciples as Jesus prayed for.]

Ac 9:17-18 Then Ananias went to the house and entered it. Placing his hands on Saul, he said, "Brother Saul, the Lord—Jesus, who appeared to you on the road as you were coming here—has sent me so that you may see again and *be filled with the Holy Spirit.*" Immediately, something like scales fell from Saul's eyes, and *he could see* again. [Paul received spiritual awakening and sight through the Divine Love as shown in an earlier chapter in this book on this passage.]

Ac 10:44 While Peter was still speaking these words, *the Holy Spirit came on all who heard the message.*

The Counsellor / Spirit of Truth / Holy Spirit

Ac 10:45 The circumcised believers who had come with Peter were astonished that *the gift of the Holy Spirit had been poured out even on the Gentiles.*

Ac 10:46 For they heard them speaking in tongues and praising God.

Explaining the background to the above, Peter said:

Ac 11:11 "Right then three men who had been sent to me from Caesarea stopped at the house where I was staying.

Ac 11:12 The Spirit told me to have no hesitation about going with them. These six brothers also went with me, and we entered the man's house.

Ac 11:13 He told us how he had seen an angel appear in his house and say, 'Send to Joppa for Simon who is called Peter.

Ac 11:14 He will bring you a *message l through which you and all your household will be saved.*'

Ac 11:15 "As I began to speak, *the Holy Spirit came on them as he had come on us at the beginning.* [outpouring of Divine Love on those of Cornelius' household as a result of hearing the salvation message.]

Ac 11:16 Then I remembered what the Lord had said: 'John baptized with water, but *you will be baptized with the Holy Spirit.*'

Ac 11:17 So if God gave them the same gift as he gave us, who believed in the Lord Jesus Christ [and his message of salvation], who was I to think that I could oppose God?"

Ac 11:18 When they heard this, they had no further objections and praised God, saying, "So then, God has granted even the Gentiles repentance unto life."

Ac 11:23 When [Barnabas] arrived [in Antioch] and saw the evidence of the grace of God [many turning to God as a result of the gospel – v. 20-21], he was glad and encouraged them all to remain true to the Lord with all their hearts.

Ac 11:24 He was a good man, *full of the Holy Spirit* [Divine Love] and faith, and a great number of people were brought to the Lord [effectiveness of a loving example].

Paul and Peter's epistles show the function and the effect of the Holy Spirit – to impart God's Love into human hearts and to bring about transformation from the human condition to divine nature.

Ro 5:5 And hope does not disappoint us, because *God has poured out his love into our hearts by the Holy Spirit, whom he has given us.*

Ro 8:5 Those who live according to the sinful nature have their minds set on what that nature desires; but those who *live in accordance with the Spirit have their minds set on what the Spirit desires* [being guided by the Divine Love].

Ro 8:6 The mind of sinful man is death, but the *mind controlled by the Spirit is life and peace*; ...

Ro 8:9 You, however, are controlled not by the sinful nature but by the Spirit, if *the Spirit of God lives in you*. And if anyone does not have the Spirit of Christ, he does not belong to Christ.
Ro 8:10 But if *Christ is in you*, your body is dead because of sin, yet *your spirit is alive because of righteousness*. ...

Ro 8:13 For if you live according to the sinful nature, you will die; but *if by the Spirit you put to death the misdeeds of the body, you will live,*
Ro 8:14 *because those who are led by the Spirit of God are sons of God.*

2Pe 1:3 His divine power [Divine Love through the Holy Spirit] has given us *everything we need for life and godliness* through our knowledge of him who called us by his own glory and goodness [God].
2Pe 1:4 Through these he has given us his very great and precious promises, so that through them you may *participate in the divine nature and escape the corruption in the world caused by evil desires.*

2Pe 1:5 For this very reason, *make every effort* [human-divine cooperation] to add to your faith goodness; and to goodness, knowledge;

2Pe 1:6 and to knowledge, self-control; and to self-control, perseverance; and to perseverance, godliness;

2Pe 1:7 and to godliness, brotherly kindness; and to brotherly kindness, love.

2Pe 1:8 For if you possess these qualities in increasing measure, they will keep you from being ineffective and unproductive in your knowledge of our Lord Jesus Christ.

2Pe 1:9 But if anyone does not have them, he is nearsighted and blind, and has forgotten that he has been cleansed from his past sins.

2Pe 1:10 Therefore, my brothers, be all the more eager to make your calling and election sure. For *if you do these things, you will never fall,*

2Pe 1:11 and you will *receive a rich welcome into the eternal kingdom of our Lord and Savior Jesus Christ.* [God's Celestial Kingdom].

Eph 3:16 I pray that out of his glorious riches *he may strengthen you with power through his Spirit in your inner being,* [soul growth]

Eph 3:17 *so that Christ [Divine Love] may dwell in your hearts through faith.* And I pray that you, *being rooted and established in love,*

Eph 3:18 may have power, together with all the saints, *to grasp how wide and long and high and deep is the love of Christ,*

Eph 3:19 and to know this love that surpasses knowledge—*that you may be filled to the measure of all the fullness of God.*

Eph 3:20 Now to him who is able to do immeasurably more than all we ask or imagine, *according to his power that is at work within us [His Divine Love],*

Eph 3:21 to him be glory in the church and in Christ Jesus throughout all generations, for ever and ever! Amen.

The next part provides further insights into the nature of the Holy Spirit and what happens to the recipients of it from both the New Testament and *The True Gospel Revealed by Jesus* volumes.

PART IV – THE HOLY SPIRIT

What Else Can We Learn About the Holy Spirit?

What else can we learn about receiving the Holy Spirit? In this Part, we'll further explore the Holy Spirit and its connection with the Divine Love. We'll also look at the relationship between God, Jesus Christ and the Holy Spirit.

Here are four insightful passages from *The True Gospel Revealed Anew by Jesus* volumes.

Yes, *you will receive that inflowing of the Holy Spirit* as they did, even while you are on earth, and will be able to *know that God is your Father* to the extent that they knew. Only you must pray more and believe more. You will not only receive that but you will also *receive power to convince men of my teachings and lead them to my Father's Love,* and also to show that you possess this Love by *being able to heal the sick by merely praying for them.* (From TGRABJ, Vol. 3, p. 43)

For correspondence with the New Testament, compare Acts 1:8: "But *you will receive power* when the Holy Spirit comes on you; and you will be my witnesses in Jerusalem, and in all Judea and Samaria, and to the ends of the earth." Also, Luke 9:1-2 states: "When Jesus had called the Twelve together, *he gave them power and authority* to drive out all demons and to cure diseases, and he sent them out to preach the kingdom of God and to heal the sick."

Back to *The True Gospel Revealed Anew by Jesus:* "*The Kingdom of Jesus will be one where only those who believe in his teachings of truth and have received the Holy Ghost in their souls, will live.* At some time, known only to God, the entrance to this Kingdom will be closed, and all who have not qualified themselves, or rather who have not striven to heed and obey these truths, and have not received this love, will not be permitted to enter this Kingdom. Those who remain outside will have the love and care of God necessary to make them comparatively happy, but will not have that supreme Love, which they can all now get if they will seek and believe." (From TGRABJ, Vol. 3, p. 111)

This passage is reminiscent of the Parable of the Ten Virgins that Jesus shared in his teachings (Matt 25:1-12):

Mt 25:1 "At that time the kingdom of heaven will be like ten virgins who took their lamps and went out to meet the bridegroom.
Mt 25:2 Five of them were foolish and five were wise.
Mt 25:3 The foolish ones took their lamps but did not take any oil with them.
Mt 25:4 The wise, however, took oil in jars along with their lamps.

Mt 25:5 The bridegroom was a long time in coming, and they all became drowsy and fell asleep.

Mt 25:6 "At midnight the cry rang out: 'Here's the bridegroom! Come out to meet him!'

Mt 25:7 "Then all the virgins woke up and trimmed their lamps.

Mt 25:8 The foolish ones said to the wise, 'Give us some of your oil; our lamps are going out.'

Mt 25:9 "'No,' they replied, 'there may not be enough for both us and you. Instead, go to those who sell oil and buy some for yourselves.'

Mt 25:10 "But while they were on their way to buy the oil, the bridegroom arrived. The virgins who were ready went in with him to the wedding banquet. And the door was shut.

Mt 25:11 "Later the others also came. 'Sir! Sir!' they said. 'Open the door for us!'

Mt 25:12 "But he replied, 'I tell you the truth, I don't know you.'

The lamp is symbolic of each person's soul, the oil represents the Holy Spirit / Divine Love, and those barred from entering the wedding banquet (Celestial Kingdom) lacked sufficient soul development in the Divine Love.

Another passage from *The True Gospel Revealed Anew by Jesus* says this: "I do not know of any mortal who has been so blessed in his earth life. *Even we who were called by him when on earth were not so blessed, until we received the Holy Spirit at Pentecost, as you are now doing*. You will receive this Great Gift in greater abundance in a short time, and then you will realize what the gift of the Divine Love means to your soul and to your happiness on earth.

So, you are now my brother and a new apostle of the Master, and I know *your work will be greater in extent than was the work of any of us when we were trying to spread his teachings while on earth*. I hope that God will bless you abundantly and keep you free from all sin and error.

I am with you very frequently, trying to help you to obtain the Divine Love of the Father.

Well, *you will receive it, and when you do, as you say, all other things will come to you - I mean all things necessary to carry on the work that has been assigned to you. So with all my love and blessings, and the assurance that you will soon receive the Love in increased abundance and do this Great Work with a faith that will not falter.* (From TGRABJ, Vol. 2, p. 112)

Again, there are two corresponding Bible passages: John 14:11-12 says: "Believe me when I say that I am in the Father and the Father is in me; or at least believe on the evidence of the miracles themselves. I tell you the truth, anyone who has faith in me will do what I have been doing. *He will do even greater things than these*, because I am going to the Father."

What Else Can We Learn About Receiving the Holy Spirit?

Acts 1:8 states: "But you will receive power when the Holy Spirit comes on you; and you will be my witnesses in Jerusalem, and in all Judea and Samaria, and to the ends of the earth."

One more time, back to *The True Gospel Revealed Anew by Jesus*.

Being "born again" is the flowing of the Holy Spirit into the soul of a man and the disappearing of all that tended to keep it in a condition of sin and error. It is not the workings of the man's own will but the Grace of God. It is the Love of God that passes all understanding. You will soon experience the change, and then you will be a happy man and fit to lead others to the truths of God. Let your heart be open to the knockings of the Spirit, and keep your mind free from thoughts of sin. Be a man who loves his God and his fellow man. Your love is only now of the earthly kind, but it will soon be of the things spiritual.

You must not let the cares of this world keep you from God. *Let His Spirit come into your soul. Your will is the thing that determines whether you will become a child of God or not. Unless you are willing to let the Holy Spirit enter into your heart, it will not do so.* Only the voluntary submission to or acceptance of the Holy Spirit will make the change." (From TGRABJ, Vol. 2, p. 2).

In summary, receiving the Holy Spirit is the prerequisite to entering God's Kingdom. It is the key to being born again, wherein the person's soul is cleansed from sin and error. This all is a great blessing and occurs by God's grace. It will not happen without each person's desire. The new birth makes us true children of God and we'll know that God is our Father.

Receiving the Holy Spirit imparts power to do God's work – to disseminate Jesus' teachings and lead people to the Father's Love and His kingdom. Today's ministry of preaching Jesus' gospel is more powerful than what Jesus and his disciples were able to accomplish while on earth.

Holy Spirit and Divine Love

The Holy Spirit is God's instrument to impart divine love and nature into human souls (Rom. 5:5), transforming the soul from just a divine image into divine substance. The Spirit is eternal and omnipresent, but is *not* God or a part of a divine trinity. Also referred to as the Comforter, it is the spirit of truth, love, life, hope, holiness, and adoption – making humans into true children of God.

Additionally, in the Bible, the Holy Spirit has the following descriptive titles: the Spirit of grace, the Spirit of wisdom and understanding, the Spirit of counsel and might, the Spirit of knowledge and of the fear of the Lord, the Spirit of promise, the Spirit of glory, and the Spirit of power, love, and a sound mind. It is also spoken of as the Spirit of God the Father, Spirit of the Lord, and the Spirit of Christ. (See Psalm 139:7-10; Isaiah 11:2; Matthew 10:20; 28:19-20; John 15:26; Acts 5:3-4, 9; Romans 1:4; 5:5; 8:2, 9, 15; Hebrews 10:29; 2 Timothy 1:7.)

It is possible that some of the above descriptors refer to God's Spirit rather than the Holy Spirit, which is the part of God's Spirit that exclusively conveys the Divine Love into human souls. The Holy Spirit is God's messenger for this purpose and is not God's creation, as is Jesus and the rest of humanity. It is merely an energy of the soul of the Father, conveying His Love. The Spirit is not a separate entity but is entirely dependent upon the powers of the Soul of the Father for its existence.

By contrast, God's Spirit demonstrates to humans the operation of God's Soul in other directions and for other purposes. His creative spirit, His caring spirit, and the spirit maintaining the operation of the universe through God's laws and designs are not the Holy Spirit. They are, however, equally a part of God's Soul and necessary for the manifestations of God's powers and the exercise of the energies of His Soul. Dealing with matters of the universe, they are not involved in the interrelationship between the Soul of God and human souls.

(References for the above part are TGRABJ, Vol. 2, p. 231; and Vol. 1, p. 72.)

Holy Spirit References as Divine Love References

As God's instrument which imparts the transforming divine love and nature into the souls of those who desire and pray for it, the Spirit acts as a bridge between the believer and God the Father. In the Bible, in many instances, the *Holy Spirit can be seen as synonymous with the Divine Love*.

With the above in mind, we can learn the following about the Holy Spirit / Divine Love: It is always with God's children and communicates to them the deep things of God, which of and by themselves they could not understand. It dwells in believers' souls and imparts the qualities listed as the fruit of the Spirit – love, joy, peace, patience, kindness, goodness, faithfulness, gentleness, and self-control. It guarantees both the present status as a child of God and a future inheritance in the kingdom of God (Celestial Heavens). Those born of the Spirit (born anew through the Divine Love) become heirs of God and co-heirs with Jesus Christ – who was the first to be born in this way. Finally, through the Holy Spirit / Divine Love, God's divine substance comes to dwell in the soul of the converted (transformed, born anew) person. (See John 3:5-8; 14:20-23; 16:13; Romans 8:15-18; 1 Corinthians 2:9-12; Galatians 4:6-7; 5:22-25; Ephesians 1:13-14; Hebrews 13:5.)

In addition, the Spirit is described in the following ways, which could also apply to the Divine Love / nature, or promptings from God Himself. It strives, convicts, directs, teaches, helps, intercedes, and inspires. It also manifests as a power that anoints, renews, fills a person, and is given or poured out as a gift. (See Genesis 6:3; Luke 1:15, 41, 67; 12:12; John 14:16-17; 16:8; Acts 2:38; 10:38, 44-45; 11:15; 13:2-4; Romans 8:26; Titus 3:5; 2 Peter 1:21.)

Holy Spirit Analogies as Applicable to Divine Love

Several physical analogies for the Holy Spirit in the Bible illustrate its characteristics and abilities – which again would also apply to the Divine Love. These include water, fire, wind (or breath), and oil. Analogous to water, the Spirit revives those who were dead in sins, washes away sins, brings about spiritual growth, and is essential for eternal life. Akin to fire, the Holy Spirit purifies hearts, transforms minds, and gives spiritual enlightenment. Similar to wind or breath, the Spirit sustains life. Comparable with oil, the love and uniting power of the Holy Spirit smooth friction among people. (See Matthew 25:1-13; John 3:8; 7:38-39; 14:12; Acts 1:8; 2:2-4; Romans 8:9-11; 12:2; 1 Corinthians 6:11; 2 Corinthians 1:3-4; Ephesians 1:17-19; 2:1-5; 2 Thessalonians 1:8; 3:12; 1 Peter 1:21-23; 2 Peter 3:18.)

Work of the Holy Spirit / Divine Love in Believers

The Bible speaks of individuals being called or drawn by God. This drawing awakens interest in the things of God, convicts people of having come short of God's requirements (which is sin), and leads them to repentance and turning to God (conversion). When the soul is thus open and receptive to the Divine Love, the Holy Spirit imparts God's love and nature, and the believer becomes a new creation. This progressively results in a new perspective on life and how it is lived – in Bible language, walking in the Spirit and being at one or in harmony with God. (See John 6:44, 63; Acts 2:38; 5:32; John 14:16-17, 26; 1 Corinthians 6:17; 2 Corinthians 5:17; Ephesians 2:1-7; 2 Peter 1:4.)

The Holy Spirit / Divine Love fills the hearts / souls of believers, empowering them to overcome the downward pulls of human nature and ultimately to do even greater works than Jesus did while on the earth. The Spirit helps Christians as a comforter, counsellor, and intercessor, and also provides the assurance of adoption as children of God. They are led into deeper truth and gradually transformed into the likeness of Jesus – the first recipient of the Divine Love in his soul, who gained immortality and is now the Master of the Celestial Heavens. (See John 14:16-20, 25-26; 15:26; 16:7-14; Romans 8:5-7; 13-16, 26-29; 1 Corinthians 2:13-14; 12:3; 2 Corinthians 3:18; Galatians 4:4-7; Colossians 1:15-18; Hebrews 1:6.)

Christians are to be filled with the Spirit / Divine Love – literally, to keep on being filled – and to walk in the Spirit / Love. Implied is a prayerful relationship with God and seeking to be in tune with the leading of the Spirit / Love nature within – that is, working toward having love as the guiding motivation in each area of life. No one is a true child of God without the Holy Spirit / Divine Love dwelling in them. Finally, God's children are admonished not to resist, grieve, or quench the Spirit by following their sinful nature. (See John 15:1-8; Acts 7:51; Romans 8:9-16; Galatians 5:16-25; Ephesians 4:30; 5:8-10, 18-21; 1 Thessalonians 5:15-24.)

By the power of the Holy Spirit / Divine Love within, the children of God will be raised from the dead which means being given immortality and glory when they shed the physical body at death and enter the spirit world. They will have imperishable and incorruptible bodies like Jesus Christ's body and become more and more like him in their new state as divine angels. They will then see him as he is, the one who interceded for them, and helped them during their physical lives. (See Romans 8:10-18; 1 Corinthians 6:11; 15:51-57; 2 Thessalonians 2:13; 1 Peter 1:2; 1 John 3:2.)

Relationship of God, Jesus, the Christ and Holy Spirit

What is the relationship between God, Jesus, the Christ and the Holy Spirit? After several Church Councils at time of Emperor Constantine in the fourth century, from much discussion and disputing, the bishops concluded that God the Father, Jesus and the Holy Spirit were in a "Trinity" relationship – united as three persons in one Godhead. Most orthodox Christians accept this idea by faith, even though it is hard if not impossible to understand and poses problems, such as how can God be one and yet consist of three persons, does the Bible really say that Jesus is God, and how is the Holy Spirit God?

It is beyond the scope of this book to delve into the Trinity doctrine in detail. But here are two passages from *The True Gospel Revealed Anew by Jesus* volumes that provide insights into the relationship of nature of the Father, Jesus, the Christ and the Holy Spirit.

Quoting from TGRABJ, Vol. 2, p. 2: "I [Jesus] was the instrument in God's hands of leading men to His favor and Love. When I said 'I am the Way, the Truth and the Life,' I meant that through my teachings and example men should be able to find God. I was not God and never claimed to be. The worship of me as a God is blasphemous and I did not teach it. I am a son of God as you are. Do not let the teachings of men lead you to worship me as a God. I am not.

The trinity is a mistake of the writers of the Bible. There is no trinity – only one God, the Father. He is one and alone. *I am His teacher of truth, the Holy Spirit is His messenger and dispenser of Love to mankind. We are only His instruments in bringing man to a union with Him.* I am not the equal of my Father – He is the only true God. I came from the spirit world to earth and took the form of man, but I did not become a God – only the son of my Father. You also lived as a spirit in that kingdom, and took the form of man merely as a son of your Father. You are the same as I am, except as to spiritual development, and you may become as greatly developed as myself.

When on earth, I was the only son who had, until then, become vested with the Divine Love of God to the extent of being wholly free from sin and error. My life was not a life of earthly pleasure or sin, but was given wholly to my Father's work. I was His only son in that light. He was my Father as I knew Him to be."

Continuing in TGRABJ, Vol. 3, p. 51: "... The Holy Spirit is of God and not a medium of Jesus to bring about their New Birth and entrance into God's Kingdom. He [God] is the one that confers the blessings of the Spirit and they will realize it when they receive the Spirit's inflow of Love and Grace. Yes, many have and their influence is good and helpful, their spirit friends are with them at their meetings and help them to realize that God is Love and Truth.

The Holy Spirit is the one that can cause the inflowing of God's Love and it is present in all meetings as it is without form or personality. It is the messenger of God and it can be in all places at the same time so that the penitents no matter how far apart can receive its influence and feel its saving Grace and Love. It is not necessary for it to use other spirits to carry its love and influence. *It of itself is able and all comprehending enough to influence the persons who seek for its inflowing.* So do not think that you have to have Jesus present in order to obtain the blessings of the Holy Spirit. He meant that when they are gathered together for the purpose of seeking the Love of God he would be able to help them feel the influence of the Holy Spirit, he would not have to be present himself for that purpose, but *he would be represented by the Holy Spirit.* ...

Jesus is not a spirit in the sense that God is a spirit. He is only an individualized spirit as you are. He is only a spirit of such wonderful development that he can control all the spirits of his own manner of thinking and who have been Born Again into God's Kingdom so that he can have them do his work just as he teaches them to do. Yes, *he can direct the Holy Spirit in the sense that when the penitent prays for help the Holy Spirit will respond and fulfill the work that the Father has provided it to do.*

Jesus is the truest exponent of his Father's Truths and he alone (only) through his teachings can cause the Holy

Spirit to enter the hearts and souls of mankind. ... The Father has given him the power to control all the spirits that are of the Father's Kingdom of Truth and Love.

Christ is not only a spirit of the Father, but is the one that God gave to Jesus when he anointed him on his earthly mission. He is the one spirit that cannot be made to do anything that is contrary to God's Love and Law. No, not in addition to the spirit that Jesus had, but the spirit that God gave to Jesus at the time of the anointing.

The spirit that Jesus had before that time became one and the same with the Christ Spirit - they are now one - *Jesus is not a man as is taught by some writers, but is the Christ of God – a spirit that is full of God's truths.* He is the great dispenser of truths and he cannot lie nor do anything but what the Father has given him to do.

Yes, *Jesus the Spirit is only a spirit as you have a spirit, but Jesus the Christ is a Spirit that is without form or limitations, so that he can be everywhere at the same time. Yes, he meant that he as the Christ would be with all peoples wherever they might be gathered together seeking his help and teachings, but as Jesus the mere spirit, he did not mean that he would be with them.*

So you may believe that *he is with you always in the sense that he is your Christ.* It is Jesus the teacher of truth and not the Christ, the latter is with you and everyone else at all times. *Only the penitent must ask that he let them feel his influence and teach them the Truth of God, and the fact that the Holy Spirit is waiting to enter into their hearts and fill them with the Divine Love....*

... The blood of Jesus or the crucifixion is not necessary, as a matter of belief to their salvation. *The only thing that saves them from their sins and reconciles them to God is that they must become conscious of God's Truths and receive the Holy Spirit into their souls.* No vicarious suffering on the part of Jesus is necessary to save them. He never taught that erroneous doctrine and it is not doing any good by being taught by the preachers who claim to represent his cause."

In summary, God the Father is one and unique. Jesus became His first true son, as distinguished from His created son, in the sense that he was the first to receive the Divine Love – the Father's substance – to transform his soul from the image of God into the substance of God. With this he received an anointing and became the Christ.

Jesus is the first of many siblings to become a true child of God through the Divine Love. The same transforming gift is available by grace to all who sincerely desire it.

The Holy Spirit is the instrument of God that imparts the Divine Love into the hearts/souls of penitent believers who desire it. It enables soul transformation resulting in the new birth, intimate interrelationship with the Father and Jesus, and a unity – at-onement – with the Father,

Jesus and fellow believers. The new birth is the condition of entry into the Celestial Kingdom – the habitation of immortal divine angels. They live in supreme happiness and have opportunities for unlimited growth in love, knowledge and service.

PART V – ACCESSING GOD'S LAVISH GRACE

If You Understand the Gospel of Grace ...

If you have understood the main message of this book – the gospel of God's grace, preached by Jesus, and involving salvation through the new birth and heart transformation by God's Love – if you feel excited by what you have learned and the possibilities open to you, and if you desire to take God up on His amazing offer of grace, all you need to do is ask for God's Love imparted by the Holy Spirit (Rom. 5:5). You will not be turned down. Jesus encouraged:

Luke 11:9-13 "So I say to you: Ask and it will be given to you; seek and you will find; knock and the door will be opened to you. For everyone who asks receives; he who seeks finds; and to him who knocks, the door will be opened. "Which of you fathers, if your son asks for fish, will give him a snake instead? Or if he asks for an egg, will give him a scorpion? If you then, though you are evil, know how to give good gifts to your children, how much more will your Father in heaven give the Holy Spirit to those who ask him!"

So if you are ready to test the truth of the message in this book, why not commit to start praying for the Divine Love? You can use one or more of the prayers in the next chapter, or just ideas from them that resonate with you. Or simply come to God with your own heartfelt prayer. After a time of earnest and consistent prayer, you are likely to notice greater peace and closeness to the Creator, as well as more love, joy, happiness and serenity.

As you continue praying, your life will become more loving and less stressed. You'll grow in understanding of vital spiritual truths. Your relationship with God will grow and you'll be more and more conscious of His working in your life.

You will not be immune to the trials and challenges of life, but when they come, you'll be helped. Ask for strength, wisdom and assistance in difficult situations and your prayers will be answered – maybe not quite the way you wish or hope, but it will be for the best in the long run.

And when your time comes to leave this physical world and enter the spirit world, you will be well on the way to the Celestial Kingdom of God that Jesus spoke about, where he was going to prepare beautiful mansions for his disciples, and where unsurpassed bliss and happiness and unlimited growth await those who have achieved at-onement with their Heavenly Father through soul transformation from divine image into divine substance by the Divine Love.

Prayers for Divine Love

The following is a prayer given by Jesus for the receipt of the Divine Love. It doesn't have to be prayed verbatim, but it can give ideas how to approach the Father who is always happy when His children ask for His Holy Spirit which imparts the Divine Love (Luke 11:13).

In effect, the prayer contains the basic truths given to humankind by Celestial Spirits. One person used the following analogy: Praying with these words, thought by thought, is like appreciating the beauty of a crystal chandelier, many little crystals of divine truth that we behold in our meditations, and throughout our day.

This longer, formal prayer can be substituted by personal heartfelt prayers. Also, as one goes about their daily tasks and becomes aware of God during their day, brief, even non-verbal, requests expressing the soul's desire for the Divine Love can be uttered at any time or place.

The Prayer Perfect

Our Father, who are in heaven, we recognize that You are all holy and loving and merciful, and that we are Your children, and not the subservient, sinful and depraved creatures that our false teachers would have us believe. (Matthew 6:9; 1 John 4:8, 16)

That we are the greatest of Your creation, and the most wonderful of all Your handiworks, and the objects of Your great Soul's Love and tenderest care. (Psalm 139:13-18)

That Your will is that we become at one with You, and partake of Your great Love which You have bestowed upon us through Your mercy and desire that we become, in truth, Your children, through Love, and not through the sacrifice and death of any one of Your creatures. (John 17:11, 20-26)

We pray that You will open up our souls to the inflowing of Your Love, and that then may come Your Holy Spirit to bring into our souls this, Your Love in great abundance, until our souls shall be transformed into the very essence of Yourself; and that there may come to us faith – such faith as will cause us to realize that we are truly Your children and one with You in very substance and not in image only. (1 John 4:7, 12-13, 16-17)

Let us have such faith as will cause us to know that You are our Father, and the bestower of every good and perfect gift, and that only we, ourselves, can prevent Your Love changing us from the mortal to the immortal. (James 1:17-18)

Let us never cease to realize that Your Love is waiting for each and all of us, and that when we come to You, in faith and earnest aspiration, Your Love will never be withheld from us. (Luke 11:13)

Keep us in the shadow of Your Love every hour and moment of our lives, and help us to overcome all temptations of the flesh, and the influence of the powers of the evil ones, which so constantly surround us and endeavour to turn our thoughts away from You to the pleasures and allurements of this world. (Matthew 6:13; James 1:13-15)

We thank You for Your Love and the privilege of receiving it, and we believe that You are our Father — the loving Father who smiles upon us in our weakness, and is always ready to help us and take us into Your arms of Love. (Luke 15:11-32)

We pray this with all the earnestness and longings of our souls, and trusting in Your Love, give You all the glory and honour and love that our finite souls can give. Amen. (1 Timothy 1:17)

Prayers for Divine Love in the Bible

The New Testament contains several prayers for the Divine Love and related gifts:

Ephesians 1:16-19 – I have not stopped giving thanks for you, remembering you in my prayers. I keep asking that the God of our Lord Jesus Christ, the glorious Father, may give you the Spirit of wisdom and revelation, so that you may know him better. I pray also that the eyes of your heart may be enlightened *[prayer for better soul perceptions]* in order that you may know the hope to which he has called you, the riches of his glorious inheritance *[Celestial Kingdom]* in the saints, and his incomparably great power *[Divine Love that transforms our souls from divine image to divine substance and mortal to immortal]* for us who believe. That power is like the working of his mighty strength, ...

Ephesians 3:16-21 – I pray that out of his glorious riches he may strengthen you with power through his Spirit in your inner being, *[soul growth and soul perceptions through Divine Love]* so that Christ *[Divine Love]* may dwell in your hearts through faith *[Divine Love in the soul]*. And I pray that you, being rooted and established in love, may have power, together with all the saints, to grasp how wide and long and high and deep is the love of Christ, and to know this love that surpasses knowledge – that you may be filled to the measure of all the fullness of God. *[all Divine Love here]*. Now to him who is able to do immeasurably more than all we ask or imagine, according to his power that is at work within us *[this is awesome!]*, to him be glory in the church and in Christ Jesus throughout all generations, for ever and ever! Amen.

Philippians 1:9-11 – And this is my prayer: that your love may abound more and more in knowledge and depth of insight, *[prayer for growth in Divine Love and soul perceptions]* so that you may be able to discern what is best and may be pure and blameless until the day of Christ, filled with the fruit of righteousness that comes through Jesus Christ – to the glory and praise of God. [*righteousness through soul-transforming Divine Love.*]

Colossians 1:3-6, 9-14 – We always thank God, the Father of our Lord Jesus Christ, when we pray for you, because we have heard of your faith in Christ Jesus and of the love you have for all the saints – the faith and love that spring from the hope that is stored up for you in heaven [*again, Divine Love*] and that you have already heard about in the word of truth, the gospel that has come to you. All over the world this gospel is bearing fruit and growing, just as it has been doing among you since the day you heard it and understood God's grace in all its truth. [*Divine Love is a gift of grace*]

Verses 9-14 – For this reason, since the day we heard about you, we have not stopped praying for you and asking God to fill you with the knowledge of his will through all spiritual wisdom and understanding [*soul perceptions*]. And we pray this in order that you may live a life worthy of the Lord and may please him in every way: bearing fruit in every good work, growing in the knowledge of God, being strengthened with all power according to his glorious might so that you may have great endurance and patience, and joyfully giving thanks to the Father, who has qualified you to share in the inheritance of the saints in the kingdom of light [*Celestial Kingdom reached through Divine Love*]. For he has rescued us from the dominion of darkness and brought us into the kingdom of the Son he loves, *[Celestial Kingdom of which Jesus is the Master]* in whom we have redemption, the forgiveness of sins *[through praying for and receiving the Divine Love]*.

Power of Soulful Longings

As mentioned, the above prayers give ideas how to ask for the Divine Love. But the Father will respond to every heartfelt prayer, as well as soulful, even unconscious longings. We'll conclude with a few thoughts from St. John to James Padgett (TGRABJ, Vol. 2, p. 185, paraphrased):

"I heard your prayer and know that this Love is flowing into your soul and that you now have a great abundance of it. It will never fail you when you pray for it in earnestness and with real longings. It is always ready to respond to your aspirations. Have faith, and you will have the certainty of the Love seeking to come into your soul.

You are blessed to know of the existence of this Love, and that it may be yours if you desire it and pray with true longings of your soul. If you keep the consciousness of the presence of this Love continually alive, pray whenever the opportunity presents itself – even just moments when the mind may be free from business affairs – the longings, if exercised for only a moment, will bring results, for God's ear is always open and ready to respond."

Epilogue

This book has presented a fresh look at the gospel of salvation by grace offered by a loving God. If the concepts presented here resonate with you and make sense, and you put them into practice, you have an exciting spiritual journey before you and a glorious destiny to work toward.

Adherents to all major religious traditions seek to find meaning to their life, both here and beyond. Most acknowledge the existence of a Higher Power as they understand it, such as the Source of all that is. Divine Love, the essence of a loving Creator God that He offers to share with humans if they wish to receive it, transcends all religions. If these teachings are true, they can be seen as a transcendent religion and a universal way to God and salvation (as opposed to the traditional belief that people have to become Christians and accept Jesus' sacrifice as a payment for their sins before they can be saved).

In a way, the overarching teaching of the availability of the Divine Love as a means for reaching a state of at-onement with God can be integrated into many other religions. Believers of various persuasions, who already strive for a life of love, morality and ethics can adopt the concepts and through earnest prayer, have their souls transformed by the Divine Love. If and when this happens, their very partial understanding of the ultimate reality (which we all have) will also gradually grow.

Epilogue

People of different faiths hope and believe that this life is not all there is. If that's the case, it behoves all of us to gain more understanding of the next life and prepare for it here and now. I believe that seeking and growing in the Divine Love is the best answer. However, each person has to decide for themselves.

References

Books

True Gospel Revealed Anew by Jesus, Volumes 1-4 (Publisher: Foundation Church of the New Birth)

Angelic Revelations of Divine Truth, Volumes 1-2 (Publisher: Foundation Church of Divine Truth)

New Testament Revelations of Jesus of Nazareth (Publisher: Foundation Church of Divine Truth)

53 New Testament Revelations (Publisher: Foundation Church of the New Birth)

76 Sermons of the Old Testament of the Bible, by Jesus of Nazareth (Publisher: Foundation Church of the New Birth)

Websites

http://new-birth.net/

http://universal-spirituality.net

Specific References

The New Dictionary of Catholic Spirituality, article entitled "Grace" by Robert Haight (p. 452-464)

References

Denis Edwards, *Human Experience of God*, Paulist Press, 1983

"Historicity of the Biblical Exodus Story" at https://www.quora.com/What-is-the-scholarly-consensus-on-the-historicity-of-the-Exodus-story-in-the-Bible-What-percentage-of-scholars-believe-there-is-a-historical-basis-for-the-Exodus/answer/Dick-Harfield

https://new-birth.net/padgetts-messages/true-gospel-revealed-anew-by-jesus-volume-3/jesus-is-the-way-the-truth-and-the-life-vol-3-pg43/

https://new-birth.net/padgetts-messages/true-gospel-revealed-anew-by-jesus-volume-3/ann-rollins-again-writes-on-the-kingdom-of-jesus-being-closed-vol-3-pg111/

https://new-birth.net/padgetts-messages/true-gospel-revealed-anew-by-jesus-volume-2/john-gives-encouragement-to-mr-padgett-vol-2-pg112/

https://new-birth.net/padgetts-messages/true-gospel-revealed-anew-by-jesus-volume-3/ann-rollins-answers-questions-on-the-holy-spirit-and-the-heavenly-father-vol-3-pg51/

References

https://new-birth.net/padgetts-messages/true-gospel-revealed-anew-by-jesus-volume-2/st-luke-on-the-teachings-of-new-thought-vol-2-pg322/#10

https://new-birth.net/padgetts-messages/true-gospel-revealed-anew-by-jesus-volume-3/there-is-no-one-else-in-all-the-world-at-this-time-who-is-fitted-to-do-the-work-vol-3-pg328/#10

https://new-birth.net/padgetts-messages/true-gospel-revealed-anew-by-jesus-volume-2/jesus-is-not-god-but-was-sent-by-the-father-vol-2-pg2/#A1:

What is the Holy Spirit and How Does it Work

Difference Between God's Spirit and the Holy Spirit

https://new-birth.net/padgetts-messages/true-gospel-revealed-anew-by-jesus-volume-2/jesus-is-not-god-but-was-sent-by-the-father-vol-2-pg2/#A1:

https://new-birth.net/padgetts-messages/true-gospel-revealed-anew-by-jesus-volume-3/ann-rollins-answers-questions-on-the-holy-spirit-and-the-heavenly-father-vol-3-pg51/

About the Author

Eva Peck has a Christian and international background. Through Christian work and teaching English as a foreign language in several countries, she had experienced a range of cultures, customs and environments. Having lived and worked in Australia, the United States, Europe, Asia, and the Middle East, where she was also exposed to non-Christian religions and spiritual traditions, she now draws on those experiences in her writing.

Eva refers to biblical passages and other works in this book the way she has come to understand them. Having had the opportunity to fellowship with Christians from a variety of faith traditions, she also recognizes that many faith-related issues can be understood in more than one way.

Eva studied biological sciences as well as theology at the tertiary level and has a Bachelor's degree in Science and a

About the Author

Master's degree in Theology. She is also an ordained minister and a trustee in the Foundation Church of Divine Truth. She lives in Brisbane, Australia, with her husband, Alex and their cat, Blackie.

Most of Eva's books are available on Amazon and at other online outlets worldwide. Many can be downloaded as free PDFs from Eva's website, offered as a service to those who are interested and to help them on their spiritual journey.

For more information about Pathway Publishing and
Eva's other books,
see the following pages or go to
www.pathway-publishing.org.

For free downloads, go to
https://universal-spirituality.net/about/free-publications/

About Pathway Publishing

Pathway Publishing is dedicated to sharing truth and beauty by publishing books that present what is true to life and reality, as well as what is lovely and inspirational. The goal is to not only provide sound information, but also to lift the human spirit.

Pathway Publishing has a vision of helping readers on their path of enlightenment and spiritual transformation. The wisdom and experience of spiritual teachers, thinkers and visionary writers from various backgrounds and faith traditions are recognized and valued.

Books produced by Pathway Publishing include books of spiritual nature, as well as books featuring the art, photography and Czech poetry of Eva's father, Jindrich (Henry) Degen, now in his late nineties, but still creative and productive. Many were produced in cooperative effort with Eva's husband, Alex.

Spirituality

- *Pathway to Life - Through the Holy Scriptures,* Eva and Alexander Peck (2011)
- *Journey to the Divine Within – Through Silence, Stillness and Simplicity,* Alex and Eva Peck (2011)

- *Divine Reflections in Times and Seasons,* Eva Peck (2013)
- *Divine Reflections in Natural Phenomena,* Eva Peck (2013)
- *Divine Reflections in Living Things,* Eva Peck (2013)
- *Divine Insights from Human Life,* Eva Peck (2013)
- *Jesus' Gospel of God's Love,* Eva Peck (2015)
- *Abundant Living on Low Income,* Eva Peck (2016)
- *New Birth – Pathway to the Kingdom of God,* Eva Peck (2017)
- *Realities of Life — Reflections in Verse,* Alexander and Eva Peck with artwork from Jindrich (Henry) Degen

Booklet Series

- *The Greatest Love,* Eva Peck (2016)
- *Jesus Christ – a New Look at His Identity and Mission,* Eva Peck and Michael Nedbal (2016)
- *Answers to Prayer,* Eva Peck (2016)
- *The Bible as a Guide to Life,* Eva Peck (2016)
- *Fulfillment of Old Testament Types,* Eva Peck (2016)
- *The Problem of Evil,* Eva Peck (2016)
- *Life After Death,* Eva Peck (2016)
- *Salvation,* Eva Peck (2017)

- *Who and What Is God*, Eva Peck (2018)
- *Nature of Soul and Spirit*, Eva Peck (2020)
- *Discerning Truth and Divine Guidance*, Eva Peck (2020)
- *Antidote to Fear and Anxiety: Fear of God*, Eva Peck (2020)

Art, Photography and Poetry

- *Artistic Inspirations - Paintings of Jindrich Degen* arranged by Eva and Alexander Peck (2011)
- *Floral and Nature Art – Photography of Jindrich Degen*, arranged by Eva and Alexander Peck (2011)
- *Nature's Beauty: Art Photography of Jindrich Degen*, arranged by Eva and Alex Peck (2013)
- *Colour and Contrast: Artwork of Jindrich Degen*, arranged by Eva and Alexander Peck (2013)
- *Faces and Forms Across Time: Artwork of Jindrich Degen*, arranged by Eva and Alex Peck (2013)
- *Variations: Art Exhibitions of Jindrich Degen*, arranged by Eva and Alex Peck (2013)
- *Nature in Art: Artwork of Jindrich Degen*, arranged by Eva and Alex Peck (2014)
- *Spirituality in Art: Artwork of Jindrich Degen*, arranged by Eva and Alex Peck (2014)

- *Verše pro dnešní dobu (Contemporary Verse)*, Jindrich Degen (in Czech) (2011)
- *Volné verse* (Free Verse), Jindrich Degen (in Czech) (2012)
- *Artistic Kaleidoscope – Jindrich Degen*, arranged by Eva and Alex Peck (2020)
- *A Little Artistic Collage – Jindrich Degen*, arranged by Eva and Alex Peck (2020)

Some of the publications are also available as e-books. Many are downloadable for free as PDFs as a service to God's children worldwide.
See: http://universal-spirituality.net/home-2/free-publications and www.pathway-publishing.org

Pathway Publishing
Seeking truth and beauty

www.ingramcontent.com/pod-product-compliance
Lightning Source LLC
Chambersburg PA
CBHW072053290426
44110CB00014B/1660